Understanding the Fivefold Ministry

Understanding the Fivefold Ministry

EDITED BY
MATTHEW D. GREEN

CHARISMA
HOUSE

UNDERSTANDING THE FIVEFOLD MINISTRY, edited by Matthew Green
Published by Charisma House
Charisma Media/Charisma House Book Group
600 Rinehart Road
Lake Mary, Florida 32746
www.charismahouse.com

Cover design by Matthew Crow

Library of Congress Cataloging-in-Publication Data

Understanding the fivefold ministry / [edited by] Matthew Green.
      p. cm.
  ISBN 1-59185-622-1 (pbk.)
  1. Pastoral theology. 2. Gifts, Spiritual. 3. Pentecostal churches--Doctrines.
I. Green, Matthew, 1974-
  BV4011.3.U53 2005
  262'.1--dc22
                              2005007500

ISBN-13: 978-1-59185-622-1
E-book ISBN: 978-1-59979-885-1

15 16 17 18 19 — 14 13 12 11 10
Printed in the United States of America

Contents

EVANGELISTS

PASTORS

TEACHERS

UNDERSTANDING YOUR GIFTS

Contents

Beyond Novelty to Substance

DISCERNING BETWEEN NOVELTY and substance is the enduring challenge of church leadership, not to mention God's people in general. This is more needful during these first few steps inside the twenty-first century than at any time in earlier church history. It is in a quest to contribute something of substance to a subject often pursued as novelty that this book is offered. It is needed because the subject at hand has been bandied about over recent years with a certain amount of reckless abandon. It has not been a carelessness born of insincerity, but begotten whenever the ancient and proven is treated as something "new" and when attentions become fixated on perceived "revelations" rather than the timeless and substantial *realities* at the core of a matter.

In pursuit of the substantial, *Ministries Today* magazine dedicated a year's thematic focus to the fivefold ministries listed in Paul's letter to the Ephesians. The editorial team hoped to avoid the speculative and draw a bead on the purpose of the Lord of the church—Jesus—who has personally given gifts of leadership to His people for purposes the larger text defines. They are given (1) to contribute to their nurture and growth, (2) to serve their health and well-being, and (3) to advance their fruitfulness and ministry. However, in the face of the clarity of His motive, those primary foci are not always maintained in view. Throughout the last fifty years they have recurrently found an excitable audience of earnest advocates, but too seldom ones whose primary focus is on those values just outlined. And therein lies the need for more than mere *review*—there is a desperate need for *refocusing*.

The oft-designated "Ephesians 4:11 office ministries"—*apostles, prophets, evangelists, pastors, and teachers*—have been belabored in ways that have led me to resist the classic term "office ministries" frequently given them. This is because something *official* has increasingly drawn the focus away from Jesus' motive. His is the Giver of servant leaders, not the "Elevator" of people to office or position. And it is precisely at that point where a significant absence of discernment between *servant leadership* and *positional authority*…where *novelty*, instead of *rock-solid substance*, has intruded into the thought and life of today's church when these roles are discussed.

There is a starting place for regaining our focus. It's in coming back to examine Jesus Himself as the model and founder—the definer of all five roles.

1. He is heaven's sent Apostle and High Priest of our confession (Heb. 3:1).

2. He speaks as the Ultimate Prophet—the Incarnate Word Himself (John 1:14).

3. He is the original Evangelist, with Luke 4:18–19 describing how His proclamation brings salvation's multiple graces.

4. He is the Great Shepherd (Pastor), who laid down His life for the sheep (Heb. 13:20).

5. He is the Teacher—the Consummate Rabbi who alone has the words of eternal life (John 6:68).

In all these manifest roles, to look at Jesus is to be struck with dominating qualities.

- *Jesus never struggles for position*, but generates the trust and following of *disciples* more by reason of His character than by the exploits of His public persona or ministry. *Crowds* may follow "ministry," but the church will be ultimately shaped by *disciples* He shaped with a depth of character that produced leaders who would provide continuing foundational qualities to transmit to generations forthcoming.

- *Jesus is distinguished by what He gives of Himself,* not what He gets for Himself. He never asserts a quest for control but instead gives Himself to see people released; He never seeks power, but through His own submission to the Father functions with an authority that drives back the darkness and brings the bound and blinded into the light. His model distinguishes between *turf building* and *extending God's Kingdom* with clarity, most of all by His own self-sacrificing ways.

Further features of His model could be presented, but those two are sufficient to make the point. When the *substance* of God's "Word-defined" manifestation of all the Ephesians 4:11 ministries is seen incarnated, and assessed by weighing how our Lord reveals Himself, the cheapness of the mere novelty in today's frequent preoccupation with power and position, rather than serving, assisting, and releasing those one leads, is shone up as mere novelty.

It is in hopes of refocusing the real and dismantling the merely novel—the *novel* being seen in ideas and applications that become proposed and pursued as though they are *something new,* as *a new-era revelation to the church,* or as *central to a last-days move of God*—that we offer this compilation of articles.

We trust they will help where definition is needed so that refocus may be realized. But more than anything, we hope they might draw us all to the feet of the Giver of these servant roles. Because if we will position ourselves there—always bowed very low and always mindful it is from that stance our leadership will alone remain untainted by the subtleties of pride and temptation to power-seeking—we will have found the true key to dynamic "last days" leadership. It's rooted in knowing Him, who "emptied Himself of all but love" and who "came not be ministered unto, but to minister, and to give His life a ransom for many."

—JACK W. HAYFORD
PRESIDENT, FOURSQUARE CHURCH INTERNATIONAL
CHANCELLOR, THE KING'S COLLEGE AND SEMINARY

Introduction

—Matthew Green

MAYBE YOU ALREADY have your mind made up about the fivefold ministry. I know I did. I, for one, had a hard time swallowing the suggestion that there are modern-day apostles and prophets (even though I had no problem accepting the existence of modern-day evangelists, pastors, and teachers).

But in editing the articles for the focus on the fivefold ministry that we featured in 2004 in *Ministries Today*, I had a change of heart—and mind. It wasn't so much the well-articulated arguments as it was the stories—stories that reminded me of accounts from the Book of Acts and the first three centuries of church history.

In the following pages you'll read some of these stories and some intelligent discussions on apostolic accountability and prophetic balance. You'll also read about the need for fire-filled evangelists, sound teachers, and healthy pastors. We hope that, in the mix of interviews, profiles, and teachings, you'll discover that the fivefold ministry is alive and well in the church today—and you'll come to a better understanding of how these ministry gifts equip the body of Christ for maturity and mission.

Ultimately, you may find your own place among the fivefold ministry—not a position of authority and power, but one of effective service in a kingdom that is advancing at a pace never before seen in history. May you be humbled as you find your place in this kingdom.

> Therefore, since we are receiving a kingdom that cannot be shaken, let us be thankful, and so worship God acceptably with reverence and awe, for our "God is a consuming fire."
> —Hebrews 12:28–29, NIV

About the Author

Matthew D. Green served for four years as editor of *Ministry Today* magazine. He is currently a freelance writer and director of communications for Pioneers, a mission agency supporting more than one hundred eighty church-planting teams among unreached people groups in eighty-two countries. His Web site may be found at www.matthewdgreen.com.

CHAPTER 1

Apostles Among Us

EVEN THOUGH THEY hold pride of place in Paul's Ephesians 4 list, apostles are the most controversial of the five, and everyone in the Charismatic/Pentecostal community seems to have an opinion about who is an apostle, who is not, and why you should read their latest book on apostleship. The apostle debate shows no sign of losing steam, but we think you'll agree that the leaders highlighted in the following pages demonstrate the key characteristics embodied in the New Testament's description of apostolic ministry.

Each demonstrates humility and servanthood, intent not on building a personal empire, but on equipping and releasing others for effective ministry. Each received a dramatic call and possesses unique gifts as a pioneer in his or her arena of ministry. Each has experienced signs and wonders in the wake of his or her ministry. Each is passionately committed to sound theology, both in its practical and doctrinal expressions.

We hope that as you read, you'll agree: apostles are among us today. And their ministry is crucial for the equipping of the body of Christ and the evangelism of the nations in the twenty-first century.

TO EUROPE WITH LOVE
—MATTHEW GREEN

Samuel Lee was looking for something to believe in when he immigrated to the Netherlands from his native Iran. A disenchanted Muslim, Lee studied sociology at the University of Leiden and became fascinated with the writings of Karl Marx and Friedrich Engels, ultimately embracing the atheistic doctrines of communism. A verbally aggressive ideologue, Lee mocked and criticized anyone who attempted to share Christ with him. Nearly twenty years later, Lee has planted nineteen churches around the world, mentors one hundred fifty pastors in eighty-five nations, and leads a multicultural congregation of three hundred in Amsterdam.

The change occurred when he met Sarah, a Korean woman and a dedicated Christian. Even as Lee mocked Sarah and others who witnessed to him, God spoke to her and said, "Though he's not a Christian, he will be your husband, and in the future I'm going to use him." The two were married, and while on their honeymoon, Lee heard a voice in his room one night saying, "I am standing at the door of your heart, knocking." Responding to this dramatic call, Lee was immediately baptized in the Holy Spirit and began to speak in tongues. Then the voice said, "Go back to the world and proclaim that I am alive and am coming back."

An immigrant himself, Lee had a desire to reach expatriates living in Amsterdam and launched a ministry among African immigrants there. "When I look at the great men in the Bible, I see that the majority of them are migrants: Abraham, Jacob, Joseph..." he explains. A speaker of seven languages (including French, German, Dutch, Persian, and Turkish), Lee is well suited to lead in the multicultural environment that Western Europe has become.

"I'm going to do something great in Europe," God told Lee at a point in his ministry when some were suggesting Lee move his base of operations to the United States. Many may view Amsterdam as the axis of moral decay in Western Europe, but Lee sees it as a hub of world evangelism in Europe and beyond.

He believes that the key to this coming revival is the growing number of Christian immigrants living in Amsterdam and other European cities, working in diverse roles, from diplomats to housecleaners. "When you reach Amsterdam, you reach the world," he says. "The fact that I am based here is a privilege from the Lord."

But the Dutch capital is not the only city that has become a haven for immigrants seeking political asylum, employment, or religious freedom. Lee provides guidance for a network of forty African and Filipino churches in Athens, leaders in London and Cyprus, and countless East Asian and Sri Lankan Christians living and working in Middle Eastern nations where traditional missionaries are forbidden to enter.

The signs, wonders, and miracles that follow this unconventional missions force are hard to argue with: from a professional violinist with skin cancer who was given a clean bill of health by his doctors, to infertile couples blessed with children, to occultists delivered from spiritual bondage.

While preaching in Africa, Lee became concerned when it was rumored that local Muslims were upset with his ministry and were planning to riot. His worst fears seemed to be turning into reality as a group of men rushed to the platform during one of his services. Instead, he discovered that a crippled man in the back row of the service had gotten out of his wheelchair—healed—and others were crowding forward for prayer.

Lee is tireless in his efforts to encourage, mentor, and recruit pastors, and many of them look to him—not as an ecclesiastical supervisor, but as a spiritual father. "I say to them, 'You know me as a preacher; now get to know me as a friend,'" he explains. "I'm not there to penetrate their churches and ministries. I'm there to serve them."

"For Samuel Lee, the virtue of integrity is a crucial and fundamental component of an apostle's life in following Christ, and also important to model to those who follow him," says Gerhard Worm, a pastor in Nijmegen, the Netherlands. "The word that Samuel Lee preaches and teaches, he lives," says Carlos Villanueva Jr., a pastor on the island of Cyprus. "He is what he speaks."

A *CELLULAR* CALL
—JENNIFER LeCLAIRE

It all started with eight people in Pastor César and Claudia Castellanos' living room in Bogotá, Colombia. Twenty-one years later, the movement that was spawned in those humble circumstances has changed the dynamics of local churches in the United Kingdom, South America, and beyond. As Castellanos recalls, a prophetic word was given during the meeting, encouraging the group to "dream, for dreams are the language of My Spirit."

The results of the dreams? "The church that you will pastor will be as numerous as the stars of the sky," was the promise. "Or like the sand in the ocean, and whose number no one will be able to count." Now, Misión Carismática Internacional (MCI or International Charismatic Mission) reports forty-eight thousand cell groups composed of five to fifteen people each, with nine services per week in a stadium in Bogotá that seats eighteen thousand. In 2001, Castellanos planted a sister church in Miami that now runs approximately fifteen hundred and meets on the campus of Florida International University.

Although in his early ministry Castellanos adopted the cell-church principles taught by Korean pastor David Yonggi Cho, it was not until 1990 that he believes God began to reveal to him the unique cell-church model now known as the "G12 Vision" or "Government of Twelve." Based on the biblical account of Jesus and His disciples, the G12 model works to engender accountability, submission, and spiritual maturity through groups of twelve—each of whom are accountable to a leader and each of whom will eventually lead a group of twelve themselves.

"I began to see Jesus' ministry with clarity," Castellanos says. "The multitudes followed, but He didn't train the multitudes. He only trained twelve, and everything He did with the multitudes was to teach the twelve." This model has allowed Castellanos to reproduce himself many times over, not only through the structure of the churches in Colombia and Miami, but also through the numerous churches worldwide that have duplicated the G12 model.

While the model is not without its critics who suggest that—in the wrong hands—it breeds authoritarianism, many pastors who have implemented it have charted dramatic growth in their churches. One of these churches is six-thousand-member Jubilee Christian Center in San Jose, California, pastored by Dick Bernal, who believes God gave the idea to Castellanos because of his willingness to risk. "César feels he would be in deep, deep sin if he did not obey God no matter how wild it seems to be to the natural mind," Bernal says. "He and his wife are 100 percent sold out to the will of God even when it's uncomfortable and costly."

Although Castellanos is convinced that the G12 model will work anywhere, he continues to be committed to adapting it as times change and revises his books to tackle challenges to the G12 vision as they arise. "Yesterday's revelation is like stale bread," he explains. "But truth comes as a progressive revelation." The effects of Castellanos' vision have been felt beyond the confines of the church, and both César and his wife have sought to transform their nation on a governmental, as well as spiritual, level by running for political office and launching the National Christian Party.

Colombian president Alvaro Uribe attends one of the cell groups at MCI in Bogotá and spoke at a conference at the church earlier this year. In a nation often at the crossroads of the international war on drugs, political involvement can be more of a risk than one would think, however. On their way home from church one Sunday in 1997, César and his wife, Claudia, were attacked in their car. Both were wounded by multiple shots fired into the car, and César remained in a coma for two weeks until his miraculous recovery.

In spite of Castellanos' connections with the power brokers of his nation and church leaders worldwide, those who know him best say his greatest joy comes from seeing people's lives changed. "I've seen him with famous evangelists, and I've seen him with brand-new born-again believers," Bernal says. "He treats everybody the same. César's love for God shows in his love for people."

A SERVANT OF ALL
—JACKSON EKWUGUM

Mosey Madugba learned servanthood the tough way. "My father sent me up the river to Bane in Ogoniland to try me in the field as a missionary," he recalls. Just a teenager then, he underwent a tortuous nine-hour canoe ride, then trekked through a thick rain forest for several hours before arriving at his mission post in Bane, a community in the Niger Delta area of Nigeria.

Now, Madugba has devoted his life to training young people as he was trained for evangelism and church planting. "Once youth catch the vision, they will right the wrongs of the past," he says. "I am going for the younger generation. I want to bring them from every part of the world, spend time with them, and pour my life into them. That way they can multiply what I am doing and excel beyond what I have ever known or done."

After his missions term in Bane, Madugba attended university to pursue a degree in accounting. Then, in 1981, he joined Scripture Union as an accountant—fulfilling his one year of mandatory service required of university graduates. Madugba continued to serve as traveling secretary for Scripture Union for nine years until he felt the call to evangelize and plant churches once again. In 1991, Madugba founded Spiritual Life Outreach, a missions ministry that serves as an umbrella organization to several other ministries.

The Ministers Prayer Network, which Madugba founded in 1996, is Africa's foremost nondenominational gathering of ministers and church leaders and draws participants from Anglican, Presbyterian, Pentecostal, and Charismatic church groups. Launched in 1991, West Africa School of Missions has as its goal to train missionaries specifically to evangelize the Arab world and other areas where Christianity is threatened by Islamic militancy. "Their mandate," he explains, "is to first discover whatever Islamic stronghold exists in that area, address it in prayer, and then raise nationals to mobilize the church to respond appropriately."

The Wailing Women is a group of intercessors led by Mosey's wife, Gloria. These women travel throughout Africa and the world praying for revival and encouraging the church. Through the various ministries he leads, Madugba has mobilized leaders in seventeen countries, including Congo, Gabon, Ghana, Cameroon, Liberia, Brazil, and Argentina.

While committed to the needs in Africa and other developing nations, Madugba often comes to the United States—at his own expense—to pray for spiritual renewal. It is Madugba's belief that the church in many nations has been weakened by compromise and division—making it vulnerable to the attack of false teachings, idolatry, and the occult.

Recently, Spiritual Life Outreach has launched a program aimed at recruiting, training, and discipling young people for leadership in world missions. At last count there are groups in fifty of Nigeria's universities, and three thousand students attended a prayer and missions conference in July, where Madugba challenged them to embrace the task of global evangelism. The vice chancellor of the University of Nigeria, Nsukka—where the conference was held—was so impressed with the quality of the program that he requested Madugba to put together a leadership course for his deans and heads of departments.

After the conference, some of the students were sent to neighboring West African countries, such as Togo, Ghana, and Cameroon, where they will plant new churches and train the youth of those countries to take over the work when they return. While he has seen incredible success in recent years, those closest to Madugba know him first as a servant. Recently, fifteen thousand church leaders from thirty countries attended the Ministers Prayer Network's International Prayer and Leadership Conference, which Madugba hosted in Port Harcourt, Nigeria.

Some of the delegates were having difficulty unloading their luggage from a car and taking it into the conference hall—that is, until an unnamed baggage boy helped them. They were shocked later when they discovered that the "baggage boy" was none other than Madugba. "Servant leadership is the only leadership example that Christ left for us," he says. "What counts is not how many people serve you, but how many people you serve as a leader."

AN UNKNOWN SOLDIER
—J. LEE GRADY

Zhang Rongliang does not look like a leader of ten million Christians. Wearing unkempt navy trousers and a wrinkled blue shirt, his black hair tousled, he easily blends into the crowd when mingling among the millions in China's Henan province. But Zhang (affectionately known as "Brother Z" to those who work with him in the Chinese underground church) is no ordinary peasant from Henan.

This simple man—who prefers to sit on the floor when meeting with his team—is an apostle who has planted thousands of churches since the early 1970s, and foreign missionaries and Chinese-church workers alike consider him the most influential leader in the church in China. Like a New Testament apostle, Zhang bears the brand marks of suffering. But he also has seen New Testament–style miracles.

Converted to Christ in 1963 at age thirteen, Zhang attended covert "house churches" in rural areas of Henan—where Mao Tse-tung's dreaded Public Security Bureau (PSB) officials were on the lookout for religious "counterrevolutionaries." In 1974, PSB officers handcuffed him and beat him with sticks to force him to reveal information about his Christian activities. His refusal to deny his faith or betray his colleagues landed him in the Xi Hua labor camp for seven years.

Yet like the apostle Paul, Zhang's faith thrived even while he was imprisoned. He was put in charge of a work team and given unusual freedom to move around the camp's outskirts. As a result, he actually planted churches among rural villagers during his detainment. Zhang has been jailed four times. He has endured beatings with iron rods and bayonets. He was even shocked with an electric cattle prod.

Chinese church leaders today view Zhang's years of persecution as a badge of honor. In fact, many in the underground do not trust those who have not suffered in one form or another. They trust Brother Z. After Zhang was released from Xi Hua in 1980, he founded the Chinese for Christ movement—a vast network of churches that had grown to an estimated ten million members by the year 2001. "It is impossible to know the accurate number," Zhang says. "It's like the census of China. You can never be sure. Even while we are talking here, we are starting churches. The work of God's kingdom is so fast."

Much of this explosive growth has been linked to miracles, Zhang says. In

1993, in one rural county of Henan province, about fifteen thousand people were added to the church when news spread that a local government official was paralyzed for several hours after he tried to stop Zhang and his team from conducting an evangelistic crusade in a sports arena.

"The man pointed to us and told his deputies to arrest us," Zhang says. "But after that he could not move, and his deputies had to take him to his car even while his arm was still pointing." The officer asked Zhang to come to his office after the campaign. "When we visited him he was still paralyzed in the same position," Zhang says. "Then the officer said: 'Please forgive me. I am so sorry. Please give me a Bible. I want to become a Christian.'"

Zhang's passion, besides planting new churches, is keeping the existing congregations healthy. He says the underground church's most serious challenge today is not persecution (which seems only to trigger more growth) but heresy—caused by a lack of Bibles and trained pastors. "The need is always greater than the supply. We need about seven million Bibles a year," he says, calculating the number based on exponential growth estimates. Zhang estimates that less than half the Christians in house churches have complete Bibles, making those without Bibles vulnerable to divisive, pseudo-Christian cults.

Zhang's ministry is marked by an absolute assurance that China will be completely evangelized. Rather than cowering in the face of resistance from the government, he views barriers as opportunities. "Someday the Chinese church will go out of China to preach God's Word," says one church-planter who works closely with Zhang. Zhang has planted this same apostolic fervor in the hearts of all his leaders. Whether he lives to see China evangelized in his lifetime or ends his days in a Chinese prison, this man will remain one of the brightest lights in modern Christianity.

GOD'S FIRE ON ICE
—MATTHEW GREEN

Nineteen-year-old Kayy Gordon was sitting in her church in downtown Vancouver, British Columbia, when she received a vision of herself preaching the gospel to native peoples in the windswept tundra. More than fifty years later, the Nunavut territory of northern Canada is sprinkled with churches planted by Gordon and now led by the national pastors she trained. "It was God working," she says—almost bewildered. "I had so little to do with it—I just happened to be in the right place at the right time."

The only Christian influence the Inuits of northern Canada had before Gordon's arrival was a handful of Catholic and Anglican churches. One or two were evangelical, but, as Gordon explains, "Their message was clouded by tradition and ritual." Historically sensitive to spiritual realities, the native peoples' interest in the supernatural had been smothered by the influence of civilization. Alcoholism, drug use, and family breakup were epidemic.

Gordon crisscrossed the ice-bound territory, initially with dogsleds, then with snowmobiles, and later in small airplanes, preaching the gospel and training converts to lead new churches. Only thirty thousand people occupy the sparsely populated Nunavut territory, a land mass the size of Western Europe, primarily living in villages separated by hundreds of miles of roadless wilderness.

Called to ministry at a time when women were typically relegated to the nursery, Gordon initially encountered resistance in her home church to her call to preach. But in northern Canada, it was her commitment to the Pentecostal message that caused an Anglican bishop to try to kick her out of the village in which she was working. "They looked at me more as a threat because of the message I brought," she explains. "They didn't see that we were all on the same team."

Gordon still marvels at the hunger of the native people for the gospel—and God's response to that hunger. Miraculous healings, deliverance from drugs and alcohol, and family restoration were regular occurrences among the new believers. To this day, signs and wonders characterize the ministries of the churches Gordon planted, as indigenous pastors embrace the calling to build the church in the Nunavut territory. People have been freed of long-term strongholds—or "sins of civilization," as Gordon calls them. "Now, the Christians have the best jobs in town and positions of influence," she says.

Recently, there have been efforts to revive shamanism—the traditional practices of witchcraft and sorcery—in the villages of northern Canada. But Gordon notes that Christians in the villages gave themselves to fasting, prayer, and seeking God. "Every time," she says, "the rise of the shaman has been defeated."

Although still the president of Glad Tidings Arctic Mission, Gordon has adjusted her role from leading and supervising ministry in the nineteen churches to supporting and observing it. She travels frequently from her missions base in the Vancouver area to encourage pastors, teach at the Bible school she founded in Rankin Inlet, and speak at conferences.

"They are now running with the vision," Gordon says of the Inuit pastors. "To me, that's what it's all about—to teach faithful men who will teach others.

As a missionary, I would not feel that I have completed my work if the torch of truth had not been gripped by local hands."

Recent opportunities have frequently taken Gordon to warmer climates. Although semiretired, Gordon has been invited to teach pastors in China, Taiwan, Malaysia, Singapore, and Africa.

Always practical, she recently asked her hosts in China whether they thought it would be more efficient for her to send money rather than putting the church there through the inconvenience of finding a place for her to stay and transporting her during her ministry there. Gordon was perplexed by the response: "If we have to choose between what you can give us in money and what you can bring us in teaching, we want you to come."

We're not surprised.

CHAPTER 2

The Leadershift

—DOUG BEACHAM

SUMMARY

There's plenty of room on the harvest field for both apostolic networks and traditional denominations—if they will learn from each other's mistakes and victories and avoid the extremes of independence and institutionalism.

THE CHARISMATIC/PENTECOSTAL COMMUNITY is facing a challenge—and it's not about theology, worship styles, or spiritual gifts. It all comes down to the (until recently) dry topic of church government. As our movement enters the twenty-first century, the winds of change are blowing, and there is no shortage of "weather forecasters" with predictions of either gloom or glory.

Leaders in the New Apostolic Reformation (NAR) suggest that traditional denominations be jettisoned in favor of a more biblically based ecclesiastical structure governed by modern-day apostles and prophets. Denominational leaders, on the other hand, argue that God is continuing to work through their organizations—and that they provide more effective means of accountability, education, and support to those who choose to seek ministerial covering through them.

Most on both sides of the issue agree that twentieth-century Charismatic/Pentecostal wineskins must be adapted to hold twenty-first-century wine. I believe that apostolic and denominational leaders together hold the keys to adapting leadership structures so that the church can transform culture and advance the kingdom of God for generations to come.

As a denominational leader from a historic Pentecostal denomination, and one whose heart responds to the freshness and vitality of much in the current apostolic reformation movement, I find myself working through these kinds of questions (and many more) with pastors and other church leaders across the Pentecostal/Charismatic community.

The last fifty years have been characterized by engagement—sometimes couched in strong disagreement—between Pentecostal denominations and these "independent Charismatic segments," especially the current expression through the NAR, which is the focus of this article.

In 1998 and 1999, C. Peter Wagner wrote two books recognizing an emerging church government and leadership paradigm among certain growing congregations and church movements: *The New Apostolic Churches* and *Churchquake*. He continued to study these movements and became a catalytic leader among them. His present views of this movement are found in the newly released *Changing Church*. In this book he identifies 2001 as the beginning of a "Second Apostolic Age," which he believes has the same flow of the Spirit as the first- and second-century church.

Some key elements of this "age" are described below, with observations related to denominations.

APOSTOLIC GOVERNMENT

Denominational governments are usually rooted in democracy. Authority is vested in groups, and individual authority is curtailed. Constitutions, bylaws, and conventions provide denominational government frameworks. In denominational models, pastors are often "employees" of the congregation. Their mission is to implement the local church mission. Local church authority resides with boards and committees. Denominational leaders usually function as administrators over programs, policies, and regions.

Apostolic leaders, on the other hand, believe that apostles and prophets are the foundational government structure of the church. Called by Christ, these leaders have great individual authority over their spheres of influence. Apostolic pastors cast the vision of the church and are its primary leaders. In many cases these pastors have planted the local congregations and have received a divine call to spend their lives there.

Many of Wagner's critiques of the denominational model are on target. But the apostolic model also leaves questions.

First, Wagner implies that the only relationships that engender accountability are those that are personal as opposed to institutional. I would contend that authentic relationships are not exclusively to be found in apostolic networks and may thrive even in the context of denominational structures.

Second, in spite of some advances, the issue of accountability is still not settled among apostolic networks. Their loose structure may provide a fallow breeding ground for nepotism and/or authoritarianism.

Third, by definition, *apostolic networks* are smaller groups and are less likely to accomplish what denominations can often accomplish through combined resources that involve ownership, mutuality, and accountability.

The challenge to denominations is to find ways to discover and release the principles of the apostolic, transforming relationships within their structure.

KINGDOM VISION

A denominational mind-set tends to have the following characteristics: clergy and laity distinctions, church is thought of as a "building" in a particular location, traditional church ministers are more spiritual than Christian businesspeople, the role of Christians working in the marketplace is to support those "in the ministry."

A kingdom mind-set envisions the church operating in the everyday lives of people through "workplace apostles" who influence their environment with kingdom principles rooted in Scripture. For example, Proverbs 13:22 promises that "the wealth of the sinner is stored up for the righteous."

> The challenge to denominations is to find ways to discover and release the principles of apostolic, transforming relationships within their structure.

A kingdom mind-set takes this seriously and believes this will occur through the "gate[s] of social transformation and transference of wealth," as Wagner explains in *Changing Church*. This mind-set is not about personal aggrandizement but the mutuality of wealth transfer and social transformation.

Although Wagner's view of "workplace apostles" remains controversial among some denominational leaders, it is nonetheless a mind-set change that I believe is necessary for denominations to be more effective and biblical.

TERRITORIAL VISION

From fear, competition, or rejection, churches under the spirit of denominationalism usually exclude cooperation with other members of the body of Christ. In contrast, leaders with a kingdom mind-set seek opportunities with others to accomplish God's purposes in a given territory. This is why many apostolic leaders and churches see themselves on divine assignment regarding their cities, counties, regions, and country.

There is no inherent reason why denominational churches and leaders cannot have the same apostolic call regarding their territories and still be in relationship with their larger denominational constituency. When the spirit of denominationalism is broken, freedom to accomplish the mission with all Jesus' tribes emerges.

SPIRITUAL INVASION

For many years the guru of the church-growth movement, Wagner now sees that church growth is not about the size of a local congregation but rather about developing and releasing people who impact and transform society by kingdom principles. In this sense he aligns with dominion (or Kingdom Now) theology, envisioning the church bringing social transformation by invading the realm of the demonic in all levels of society. Wagner openly acknowledges that the eschatological implications will leave questions for many denominational leaders.

While this point will remain a point of disagreement, if not controversy, I believe Pentecostal denominations need to assess the impact of our eschatology in regard to the transforming power of the gospel in society. The seriousness of this discussion will depend on whether the apostolic reformation is able to produce the social transformation Wagner envisions.

EQUIPPING PARADIGMS

Most seminaries were founded on the European academy model: knowledge, information, criticism, and preparation to serve current systems are the priority. The NAR rejects this paradigm by shifting to its version of Ephesians 4:12: "Equipping…the saints for the work of ministry." As part of this shift, several issues emerge for Pentecostal denominations: Will accredited seminaries be shaped by the same forces that shaped Protestant seminaries? What are the implications for ordination and accountability? Can theological education make the leap from transferring information to transformational impartation?

In terms of theological doctrines, apostolic leaders and churches are less interested in the nuances that define and distance us. Notably, in recent years, traditional Pentecostal denominations have also begun to embrace a more open stance toward theological differences with their evangelical cousins. Through involvement in various evangelical gatherings, many Pentecostals have become more adept at separating doctrinal essentials and nonessentials.

While I appreciate the practical aspect of Wagner's model, I see two weaknesses. First, it may intentionally reinforce Pentecostalism's anti-intellectual stereotype. Second, he contends that many in the NAR have little or no interest in systematic theology.

While appreciating that systematic theology is often not the liveliest of courses, I'm more concerned that not understanding the basics of historical and systematic theology leaves us vulnerable to repeating past theological errors. Current leaders may understand the nuances and significance of issues facing the church. But I am concerned that this model will not adequately prepare future leaders to carefully discern and communicate the historic Christian faith "once...delivered to the saints" (Jude 3).

> There is no inherent reason why denominational churches and leaders cannot have the same apostolic call regarding their territories and still be in relationship with their larger denominational constituency.

WESLEYAN HOLINESS

The final chapter may be the most surprising of all. Wagner addresses the accountability issue not by adopting legal systems but by focusing on Wesleyan holiness. He believes Wesleyan holiness provides the biblical framework for an "apostolic lifestyle" rooted in the fear of the Lord and humility. Being from a Wesleyan heritage Pentecostal denomination, I agree with Wagner's analysis. His call to renewed personal and corporate holiness, avoiding legalism and a prideful "sinless perfectionism," is exactly what is needed in all branches of Pentecostalism.

Beyond these distinctions between apostolic networks and denominational structures, the following are several observations that I believe need to be considered as Pentecostal denominations seek to learn from apostolic networks—and not repeat their mistakes:

- While Pentecostal denominations accept the reality of contemporary "apostolic and prophetic" ministries, not all accept the NAR premise that there are contemporary "offices" of apostles and prophets. Nonetheless, denominations need to find ways to identify, encourage, and recognize the "apostolic" leaders in their midst—even if we remain uncomfortable with calling someone an "apostle." This is very different from being a "denominational man." This is openness to a dynamic of the Spirit that will often rock the boat but will point the boat in the direction God has for it.

- By definition, Pentecostal denominations must be open to what the Holy Spirit is doing afresh in each age and culture. I think one way to change our mind-sets is to stop referring to ourselves as *denominations* and call ourselves *movements*. It's a small point, but language can convey mind-set change.

- Wagner is careful to say that the NAR is not a "theological" reformation. But *Changing Church* shows that it cannot help but be. The denominational concern is whether present and/or future apostles will take the NAR concepts of *revelation* and *present truth* and formulate doctrines not clearly supported by Scripture or even adopt additional scripture.

- The process of "institutionalizing *charisma*" lies at the door and presents continual challenges. Denominations must be intentional about keeping the mission of Jesus at the forefront and beware the tendency to maintain the status quo. Most denominational leaders will tell you we are doing that. I think we are prone to blind spots and need people like Wagner to shake us.

- The NAR has recognized the importance of pastors and congregations being in covenant and connected to apostolic leaders. Denominations must find ways to navigate through the complicated waters of bureaucracy and foster genuine and transforming relationships between the various levels of leadership.

What does the future hold for apostolic networks and Pentecostal denominations? This will depend on the willingness of both to keep in step with the Spirit's direction while engaging the changing needs of culture. The challenges of the future will require increasingly creative leaders who refuse to make structures sacred and exhibit the flexibility to pour the wine of ministry into the new wineskins God is making available to His servants.

ABOUT THE AUTHOR

Doug Beacham, DMin, is the executive director of church education ministries for the International Pentecostal Holiness Church. He is the author of *Rediscovering the Role of Apostles and Prophets* (LifeSprings Resources) and *Plugged In to God's Power* (Charisma House).

FOR FURTHER STUDY

Doug Beacham, *Rediscovering the Role of Apostles and Prophets*

C. Peter Wagner, *Changing Church*

CHAPTER 3

Cover Me

—S. David Moore

SUMMARY

The apostolic movement may be a key to restoring accountability and interdependence among church leaders—if it can avoid the mistakes of the past.

MORAL AND ETHICAL scandals both inside and outside the church have made accountability the Holy Grail of the twenty-first century. Citizens are calling for greater accountability from their elected officials. Stockholders are demanding more ethical responsibility from fund managers and CEOs. Congregations are seeking to rein in morally and doctrinally errant clergy.

This quest for accountability has always existed in the Charismatic/Pentecostal community—whose leaders have often fought valiantly to seek a balance between maverick-like independence and heavy-handed authoritarianism. The most recent trend to combine accountability and biblical leadership has taken shape in what many are calling the New Apostolic Reformation. A church-growth expert and the presiding apostle of the International Coalition of Apostles (ICA), C. Peter Wagner, believes one of the major moves of God in our times is the restoration of present-day apostles and prophets.

Wagner's thoughts have emerged from his observation of a new phenomenon: pastors and leaders are joining together in networks around apostolic leaders, often associated with flagship churches. These neodenominations are a fact of life in today's church, and they have enormous influence. According to Wagner, one of their key features is the accountability produced from the relationships that are formed, and he and other leaders see these developing networks as a way to address the current ethical crisis.

A BLAST FROM THE PAST

One of the most controversial and also most influential movements within the Charismatic Renewal in the 1970s and early 1980s was born out of a similar quest for accountability. There were many wonderful aspects to the Charismatic movement; however, as with any renewal, it had its share of problems. Believers often went from one Charismatic conference or prayer group to another seeking a new experience or a new teaching. Many of these were not in any church or accountable to anyone.

They read magazines, listened to tapes by the hundreds, and eagerly awaited each new book on the Spirit's renewing work. Unfortunately, many were left unchanged. As the renewal mushroomed, it was marked by a rugged individualism in some of its leaders. A number of itinerant teachers and leaders who were regular speakers at various conferences and meetings were not accountable to any organization or network. Lone rangers abounded, and moral failures were all too frequent.

Disillusioned by what they were seeing—problems much the same as today—four popular Bible teachers, Don Basham, Bob Mumford, Derek Prince, and Charles Simpson, decided to band together for mutual submission and accountability. From this association, in October 1970 emerged the Shepherding Movement, sometimes called the Discipleship Movement.

> There is a need to make sure leaders are manifesting the works of an apostle before being labeled one.

With *New Wine* magazine as a powerful mouthpiece, the four Charismatic teachers, joined in 1974 by Canadian Ern Baxter, began teaching on the importance of the local church, submission and spiritual authority, and the need for accountability. This accountability was accomplished as each believer was "covered" in a committed relationship with a personal pastor or "shepherd."

Significantly, they taught that God was restoring biblical church government, delegating His authority through the fivefold ministry offices, including apostles and prophets. What was also unique was the Shepherding Movement's call that every spiritual leader needed to be under authority before exercising his or her own spiritual authority.

The challenge and call tapped into a leadership vacuum as hundreds of leaders, many young and untrained, responded to their teachings by submitting to one of the five or a designate. Though Mumford and the other four men originally had no intention of starting local church networks, they felt responsible to lead what their teachings had created, and, so, the Shepherding Movement was born.

Each one of the five leaders pastored a group of pastors, forming networks of churches under their oversight. These networks of churches never became a formal denomination, since the goal was always to make the association relationally based. Keeping the movement organic and relational proved difficult as growth forced more organization. Many felt the Shepherding Movement had become functionally and practically a small Charismatic denomination, despite their claims otherwise.

In 1975, several high-profile Charismatic leaders accused the five of trying to take over the Charismatic Renewal and dominate the lives of their followers, charges the five always denied. Rumors abounded as many unsubstantiated allegations were made against the movement and its leaders.

The heated controversy divided the renewal for more than a decade, and the dispute was never satisfactorily resolved. Even among the five leaders there were conflicts, and Derek Prince quietly withdrew from the group in 1984. Two years later the other four broke formal ties and ceased publication of *New Wine*, ending the Shepherding Movement as an expression of the five men's shared commitment.

High Ideals

The Shepherding Movement admittedly missed many of its ideals, and its extremes are well known. In 1989, Bob Mumford offered a public apology to those hurt by the movement's teachings and practices. Charles Simpson, who leads a major segment of those who continue in the legacy of the movement, has said that human carnality won out all too often.

While many were hurt as some leaders improperly exercised spiritual authority, mostly ignored are those who benefited from the movement and those who continue in its varied expressions today. The covenant movement, led by Simpson, maintains a commitment to many of the Shepherding Movement's founding principles of accountability, covenant relationship, spiritual fatherhood, and spiritual family—principles they believe have matured and moderated over time.

What has also been missed in the rancor surrounding the Shepherding Movement's excesses is an acknowledgment that they were legitimately challenging the extreme independence and spiritual superficiality in segments of the Charismatic Renewal. They were seeking to discern their times and formulate God-ordained answers for spiritual *lawlessness*. Both Mumford and Simpson believed they were catching and riding a wave of authentic spiritual renewal. Simpson commented that "the bigger the wave, the more debris it can carry in." So, as flawed as their application might have been at times, they were convinced it was medicine Charismatics needed.

LESSONS LEARNED

Thirty years later the same ethical shallowness they were trying to confront remains. As reports of sexual and financial impropriety continue, calls for accountability echo earlier times. This is good news. For a season, the discipleship controversy made terms such as *shepherding*, *submission*, and *covering* dirty words to some. Finally, enough time has passed that they are being used again.

> What has also been missed in the rancor surrounding the shepherding movement's excesses is an acknowledgment that they were legitimately challenging the extreme independence and spiritual superficiality in segments of the Charismatic Renewal.

The terminology and vision of apostolic networks are strikingly similar to the Shepherding Movement. The same claims are made about their relational character and the accountability that results. What can emerging apostolic networks learn from the Shepherding story? Is there any wisdom to be gained from their experience that gives perspective on the fresh conversation regarding accountability?

I recently spoke to Bob Mumford and Charles Simpson to see what they had to say. Both men, older now and tempered by time and trial, are humbled by the realization that they are the only two living members of the original five Shepherding leaders. Mumford and Simpson, having felt the pain of criticism, were cautious in their assessments but very willing to share insights that might serve a new generation of leaders.

1. Seeing a spiritual truth is never enough.

According to Charles Simpson, "Believing you see something is one thing, but building something with it is another matter." He thinks he and the other four leaders had a "naïve enthusiasm" and did not fully understand what would happen once they started teaching on submission and accountability.

"If you teach something, people will come to you for it," he recalls. The momentum their teachings created caused the movement to grow beyond their ability to manage. They simply had not planned on the response they provoked. As a consequence, many leaders were vested with great authority and put in place too soon without the proper training and testing needed.

What's the point? Growth and success can sometimes be misleading, and it is easy to promise more than can be delivered. In the midst of all the excitement about new truth, people often made commitments they could not fulfill. It is very costly and demanding to apply what we believe to real life.

2. Relationships must be authentic.

Both Mumford and Simpson point out how easy it is to say that something is "relational" and yet how hard it is to make those relationships truly authentic. Many apostolic networks make the claim they are based on relationships, and thereby they are accountable to one another.

But how substantial are these relationships? Mumford and Simpson suggest that many joined their movement, submitted to the concept of submission, but had little relational connection other than occasional interaction. Some came into the Shepherding Movement just to gain legitimacy by being associated with its leaders. For these people there was no genuine relationship.

Mumford contends that "relationships must be more than functional and superficial if there is to be any kind of real accountability." Relationships require time and investment, and there are no shortcuts to maturity.

3. Structures alone will not produce accountability.

The Shepherding Movement had personal pastors, cell groups, church councils, regional presbyteries, pastors' networks, and an apostolic council, all with the aim of producing mature disciples of Jesus, but these structures alone could not produce the desired results.

In retrospect, Mumford says that spiritual *covering* worked where there were transparent relationships in which individuals wanted to be held accountable. Accountability was something that fundamentally could not be enforced or coerced—it was voluntary and an outflow of personal integrity. This is not to say there isn't value to ecclesial, adjudicating structures or councils, but accountability starts with our relationship with God, the One to whom we will one day give an account. There is no substitute.

4. Titles can be misleading.

Mumford believes the notion of him being an apostle/pastor thrust him into a role he was not able to fulfill. The title was heady but inaccurate. Mumford was a teacher, not an apostle, but it took years for him to really see it.

Simpson and Mumford believe there is a need to make sure leaders are manifesting the works of an apostle before being labeled one and that they are also evaluated by biblical standards. They caution against pride that easily follows being given title and privilege. Simpson once said: "If you are treated like a king, before long you start thinking you are one." Humility and servanthood come before title or position.

5. Remember the human condition.

No matter one's theological position on the degree of man's depravity, it must be admitted that we are deeply flawed by Adam's fall. Simpson has lamented the "carnality that power and resources brought out in some of us." Mumford wishes he had better listened to critics even when they acted uncharitably. In 1993, he apologized to one of his most strident accusers for "being blind and stubborn" during the years of controversy.

Self-righteousness and self-justification may too easily be excused and garbed in religious terms. Current leaders need to honestly admit their fallibility and potential for missing the mark. This is why accountability is so essential. These battle-tested words of wisdom can serve us today. I don't believe the cynical dictum that says the only thing we learn from history is that we don't learn from history. Both Mumford and Simpson have learned from their past, and so can we.

A CONCLUDING CAUTION

We need present-day apostles, and the New Apostolic Reformation is a genuine expression of God's renewing work in His church. However, as Simpson and Mumford note, there is great danger in *triumphalism*—seeing one's movement as the "cutting edge" of what God is doing today. This mind-set, especially if coupled with success, tends to devalue those who don't see it their way, or worse, to write off critics as old-fashioned defenders of "tradition," unwilling to embrace God's new move—the more mean-spirited and unfair the criticisms, the easier to dismiss.

These attitudes inhibit constructive dialogue and shut off any real outside accountability. Both Mumford and Simpson believe triumphalism was one reason the Shepherding Movement missed the mark. Accountability must be more than a circle of like-minded friends. We are accountable to God, to Scripture, and to the Christian story over the centuries. We are accountable to those in this "century of the Holy Spirit," which stretches back to Azusa Street. And we are accountable to the broader Christian community of our day. Taken together, accountability will be more than a buzzword; it will be a lifestyle serving the whole church, including the New Apostolic Reformation.

ABOUT THE AUTHOR

S. David Moore, DMin, is an ordained minister with The International Church of the Foursquare Gospel and the author of *The Shepherding Movement: Controversy and Charismatic Ecclesiology.*

FOR FURTHER STUDY

Ron Burks and Vicki Burks, *Damaged Disciples: Casualties of Authoritarian Churches and the Shepherding Movement*

S. David Moore, *The Shepherding Movement: Controversy and Charismatic Ecclesiology*

Flavil R. Yeakley Jr., *Discipling Dilemma: A Study of the Discipling Movement Among Churches of Christ*

CHAPTER 4

The Doc Responds
—C. PETER WAGNER

SUMMARY

Apostolic advocate C. Peter Wagner replies to the chapters by Doug Beacham and S. David Moore.

I HAVE BEEN ASKED to respond briefly to the preceding two chapters by Doug Beacham and David Moore. I am delighted to do this for many reasons, not the least of which is the fact that both men are my personal friends, and through the years we have developed high respect for one another.

I have chosen to address five topics that Doug and David bring up in this chapter. This was not easy, for both are excellent chapters dealing with extremely important aspects of apostolic ministry today. I could have chosen twenty.

HISTORY AND SIZE

Doug Beacham traces the genealogy of the New Apostolic Reformation (NAR) to the Latter Rain Movement of the 1940s. This is correct for the NAR in the United States. Globally, however, it goes back further than that. The deepest roots are found in the African Independent Church movement, which began around 1900. It would be worthy of note also that other significant connections are found in the Chinese house church movement beginning around

1976 and the Latin American grass-roots churches that became prominent around 1980.

Related to that, Doug also makes the comment: "Apostolic networks are smaller groups and are less likely to accomplish what denominations can accomplish." This also would be true for the United States, at least up to the present time. However, it would not apply to other parts of the world such as Nigeria, China, Indonesia, or Brazil, to name a few examples.

On the subject of size, the NAR is both large and rapidly growing. David Barrett, in his three-volume *World Christian Encyclopedia*, divides global Christianity into six megablocks: Roman Catholic, Anglican, Orthodox, Marginal, Protestant (which would include the Pentecostal denominations), and Independent/Neo-Apostolic (which would include the NAR).[1] The Neo-Apostolic is the largest of the non-Catholic megablocks and the only mega-block of the six currently growing faster than Islam.

ACCOUNTABILITY

Both David Moore and Doug Beacham address the issue of accountability. In fact, David says that a major reason behind the formation of the Shepherd-ing Movement was an observation on the part of their leaders concerning the extremely low level of personal accountability among Charismatic leaders of their day.

Doug doesn't say it outright, but he implies that one advantage that denomi-nations have over apostolic networks is their built-in accountability structure and that "the issue of accountability is still not settled among apostolic net-works."

This is correct. The apostolic leaders whom I know would agree with me that if we don't come out right on the accountability issue, the NAR will have a short shelf life. Having said this, the good news is that we are making excellent progress. This is an ongoing topic in meetings of the International Coalition of Apostles (ICA).

Some apostolic networks do excel in this area. Others need improvement, and they will improve. Bob Mumford's statement that "relationships must be more than functional and superficial if there is to be any kind of real account-ability" is a word in season.

SELF-APPOINTED APOSTLES

David Moore tells us that Charles Simpson "is concerned that titles are being passed around too easily today, and many are self-designating themselves as apostles." I join Charles in being concerned about this. My hope is that as the movement matures, the responsible protocol for recognizing and commissioning apostles will be more widely accepted and practiced.

I might note that there is no such thing as a true apostle who is self-appointed. God is the one who decides to whom He wishes to give the spiritual gift of apostle. Those who have the gift have received it by grace. However, this is not true of the office of apostle. The office is attained by works, not by grace.

As those who have the gift of apostle demonstrate the fruit of that gift along with the accompanying apostolic character, they will be recognized by peer-level apostles who will commission them to the office in due time.

REVELATION

Doug Beacham says, "The denominational concern is whether present and/or future 'apostles' will take the NAR concepts of 'revelation' and 'present truth' and formulate doctrines not clearly supported by Scripture or even adopt 'additional' scripture."

I would suspect that this legitimate concern arises from certain episodes in history where some who called themselves apostles (and prophets could be included here as well) actually did contend that their revelation superceded Scripture. *The Book of Mormon* might be an example.

> There is no such thing as a true apostle who is self-appointed. God is the one who decides to whom He wishes to give the spiritual gift of apostle.

However, the apostles whom I know, many of whom do receive revelation from God on a regular basis, would tremble at the thought that new truth that they receive would in any way violate the integrity and the authority of Scripture. But it is good to keep reminding ourselves of this danger, as Doug has done, in order that it may never happen.

HOPE FOR PENTECOSTAL DENOMINATIONS

Doug Beacham's excellent book *Rediscovering the Role of Apostles and Prophets*, was written to encourage primarily Pentecostal Holiness leaders and secondarily all classical Pentecostal leaders to carefully consider the phenomenon of the burgeoning apostolic movement with the purpose of seeing how these insights might be incorporated into their ecclesiastical structures.

In his article he says, "The challenges of the future will require increasingly creative leaders who refuse to make structures sacred and exhibit the flexibility to pour the wine of ministry into the new wineskins God is making available to His servants."

Those familiar with my writings on the subject will know that my hopes for old-wineskin denominations to become apostolic new wineskins are very low. However, the Australian Assemblies of God are an example of how this can happen.

The story is told in David Cartledge's book *The Apostolic Revolution*. While my realistic expectation that this might become the rule rather than an exception may be low, I do at the same time have a sincere hope that history will prove me wrong!

ABOUT THE AUTHOR

C. Peter Wagner, PhD, is the presiding apostle of the International Coalition of Apostles and chancellor of the Wagner Leadership Institute in Colorado Springs, Colorado. He is the author or editor of more than fifty books and former professor of church growth at Fuller Theological Seminary.

FOR FURTHER STUDY

David Cartledge, *The Apostolic Revolution*

C. Peter Wagner, *Apostles and Prophets: The Foundation of the Church*

C. Peter Wagner, *Changing Church*

CHAPTER 5

Speaking for God

—MATTHEW GREEN

SUMMARY

Some of the key leaders in the prophetic movement speak out on the challenges surrounding bringing accountability to the gift of prophecy—and the crucial need for its release in the church.

SINCE THE DAYS of Moses, prophets have been serving as God's messengers—and stirring up plenty of controversy along the way. Like their ancient predecessors, today's prophets aren't afraid to step on a few toes if it means speaking out what they believe God has placed on their hearts. And just as biblical prophets often went unappreciated, many modern-day prophets face disregard and outright criticism—both inside and outside the church. This is true even in the Charismatic/Pentecostal community, which embraces the continuation of the fivefold ministry but still wrestles with the practical aspects of releasing those gifts.

Cindy Jacobs, a popular author and cofounder of Generals of Intercession, argues that there is a "serious double standard" in how prophetic ministry is judged in comparison to the other fivefold gifts. And she believes it is leading legitimate prophets to squelch their gifts. "We're so critical toward the prophetic gift, yet a pastor or teacher could get up and say the same things—supposedly under the influence of the Holy Spirit—in their sermons and not have any accountability for it," Jacobs says. "The same excesses that have plagued the prophecy movement have affected the other gifts."

What are those excesses, and how should they be addressed by leaders in the body of Christ? Moreover, how can today's prophets communicate their message effectively, not just to the church but to the world around us? Money plays a key role in this issue. Similarly, the need for accountability and the presence of false and "conditional" prophecies come into play as well. With all the challenges surrounding prophetic ministry, some may suggest that it should be avoided altogether. After all, how can something so controversial be any good for the church? However, even its most vocal critics argue that the benefits prophets bring to the church far outweigh the challenges that come with this gift.

Clear Signs

For C. Peter Wagner the signs are clear that God is using modern-day prophets to an extent unmatched since biblical times. The former cessationist-turned-cheerleader for the prophetic movement cites several readily confirmed prophecies given by his friend Chuck Pierce.

During services on December 8 and 9, 2003, Pierce prophesied in relation to the war in Iraq that "the strongman that has not been found will now be found." Iraqi dictator Saddam Hussein was arrested December 13. On May 5, 2004, the day before the National Day of Prayer, Pierce prophesied that God would open the nation to prayer in an unprecedented way on the next day. He said that God would confirm this word by blanketing Washington DC, with hail. Sure enough, hail fell on May 6, the National Day of Prayer.

Wagner says that such fulfillments bring legitimacy to the movement and assure believers that God is hearing their prayers. "When something like this happens, it builds faith tremendously," he contends. "Especially when there are factors of timing and tangible things."

Few have experienced the controversy of the prophetic movement more intensely than Mike Bickle, who was pastor of Kansas City Fellowship (KCF) in Kansas City, Missouri, in 1990 when the ministry of several prophets in his church brought criticism from a group of Charismatic pastors in the city. Although the late Vineyard founder John Wimber came to assist in reconciling the various parties involved, several leaders ultimately parted ways.

Bickle cites two dramatic fulfillments of prophecies given by a former KCF prophet, who named specific dates several months in advance and stated that God would judge "the secular arena in the United States" and then judge "the church." The day the prophet predicted God would judge the secular arena (October 19, 1987) has since become known as "Black Monday," the worst single-day decline in the U.S. stock market since 1914. On the day he predicted God would judge the church (February 21, 1988), televangelist Jimmy Swaggart confessed to moral failure.

But critics of the movement suggest that such fulfillments cannot make up for numerous prophecies that never come to fruition or are unverifiable at best.

For instance, on January 10, 2004, a controversial leader in the prophetic community gave a word in response to Osama bin Laden's prediction on Arab television that the United States would experience a catastrophe within thirty-five days. The prophet stated, "In the same period that bin Laden predicted catastrophe against this nation, I shall bring him forth, I shall raise him out of his own hiding place, and I will bring him to a place of accountability."

Asked to explain the prophecy's apparent lack of fulfillment, the prophet responded that his prophecy was "interpreted incorrectly" and that "it did not specify a particular day that the thirty-five days would commence."

Mike Bickle says that prophetic ministry in the United States today is still immature in its expression and that even the most well-known prophets miss the mark sometimes. He notes that the prophet who predicted judgment of the secular arena and the church has since given several prophecies that were not fulfilled—including a time-sensitive prediction that California would be destroyed by an earthquake.

However, the fulfillments Bickle has seen have led him to exercise caution in labeling prophets as "false," even when their predictions do not come to pass. "The easy response is to discount a prophetic person who gets it wrong," he says. "That's not the right response. We have the 'horrible' job called discernment." Instead of false prophecy, Bickle identifies much that occurs in current prophetic circles as "soulish" or "humanly generated," claiming that it comes from people who are genuinely sincere, but ultimately overzealous and attention-seeking.

> The same excesses that have plagued the prophecy movement have affected the other gifts.
>
> —CINDY JACOBS

"There is a substantial amount of humanly generated activity in the name of the prophetic," he says. "Just as there is humanly generated preaching in the teaching ministry and humanly generated evangelism in evangelistic ministry. I see genuine prophetic ministry increasing radically, but the hype, human zeal, and religious enthusiasm will increase as well," he notes. "Ultimately, critics will have more opportunities to be convinced, but there will be plenty of opportunities for them to write it all off if they want to."

UNDER THE MICROSCOPE

Many argue that this human element in prophecy necessitates a commitment to examining every prophecy in light of Scripture—and ultimately pursuing some form of accountability. Michael Fletcher, pastor of the three-thousand-member Manna Church in Fayetteville, North Carolina, is an advocate of prophetic ministry, but he argues that many of the problems surrounding the prophetic movement arise when personal and prophetic experiences are elevated in authority beyond Scripture. "Whenever you allow the prophetic to interpret scriptures—a prophetic hermeneutic—then you have a whole new set of meanings and ideas that may be derived from Scripture but are not grounded in it," he suggests. "That makes us all look flaky."

Clem Ferris, a prophetic leader with Grace Churches International, based in Chapel Hill, North Carolina, agrees, suggesting that the current spiritual climate—which he describes as "apocalyptic"—sometimes creates an environment for imbalance in prophetic ministry.

"Imbalance comes from the subjective nature of the prophetic word," he says. "There is the temptation of sensationalism, not guarding against a spirit of error." His solution? "The subjectivity of the prophetic word can only be balanced by the objectivity of the written Word," he says. "Therefore, prophetic ministries today must maintain an orientation to sound and systematic theology in their own lives, while constantly being subject to the judgment of the written Word of God."

Ferris suggests that prophecy is by nature fallible and imperfect—underscoring the need for biblical scrutiny. "We must remember that we are not judging people here," he notes, "only the message and the spirit that drives it."

Fletcher agrees, citing Paul's contention that "we know in part and we prophesy in part" (1 Cor. 13:9). "That means that prophecy comes from God, but it passes through the soul of the prophet—allowing his or her impression of the word or picture to be included with the word given," he says. "If the prophet allows more of his own impression to win the day, he can misunderstand what God is trying to say—or, the listener can misunderstand what God is saying."

THE *JONAH* FACTOR

At no time is the prophetic movement more vulnerable to criticism than when its members describe events in the future that they believe will occur. Like the prophet Jonah, they find themselves in a particularly tight spot when they predict disaster with the implication that it will be averted by repentance.

C. Peter Wagner notes the instance of a well-known prophet predicting in 1998 that portions of California would fall into the ocean as the result of an earthquake. Because of the prophet's respect in the prophetic community, many responded to the message, scheduling intercessory-prayer events throughout California. While the disaster never occurred, Wagner does not question the validity of the prophecy, noting that the prediction—like that of Jonah—came with an implicit condition: "Repent, and disaster will be averted." Critics would contend that this is merely a convenient ex post facto explanation for a false prophecy, since—unlike Nineveh—there was no tangible evidence that California experienced large-scale repentance or spiritual renewal.

In the late nineties, prophetic messages abounded detailing the coming Y2K cataclysm, but many fears were debunked in 1999 long before the ball dropped in Times Square. As a result, prophecies began to take a decidedly conditional tone—highlighting the potential for disaster, but admitting that God could change His mind.

For instance, Bill Hamon, an author of numerous books on prophetic ministry, issued a "consensus of nationally known prophets on Y2K" derived from a gathering in Colorado Springs on January 28, 1999. While the report predicted minimal problems related to the turn of the millennium, it stated, "Y2K is a minor problem in comparison of what is coming later." World War III; temporary Islamic rule in America; bombs in school buses, malls, and stadiums; and destructive weather patterns were just some of the disasters predicted in the report.

> If we like someone who gives a prophecy, we don't scrutinize it like we would if the relational ties were not there.
>
> —MIKE BICKLE

However, the time frame for fulfillment was vague, and it was essentially stated in the document that these events could be averted by national repentance: "God will remove His protective covering over America unless we turn the church to righteousness and the nation back to godly ways by the end of the year 2002."

Wagner admits that there is no tangible way to verify prophecies such as these, but he believes that God uses conditional predictions to mobilize the church to prayer and intercession. "We believe that many prophecies are given to activate the body of Christ to stand in the gap powerfully enough so that God will change His mind," he explains.

GIVING ACCOUNT

According to Wagner, the challenges arising out of the modern-day prophetic movement should be solved through accountability, not suppression of the gift. "One of my concerns is that some prophets have not yet learned to handle contemporary prophetic protocol," he explains. "They're freelancers and operate on their own without the constraints of the body of Christ."

Founded in 1998 by Wagner, Cindy Jacobs, and several others in the prophetic community, the Apostolic Council of Prophetic Elders (ACPE) offers apostolic oversight and accountability for its members. "ACPE was organized on the basis that prophecies were being released without checking with others," Wagner says. "I personally detect a lot less flaky prophecy than there was a few years ago." Wagner explains that the ACPE offers both "peer-level" (prophet to prophet) and apostolic (apostle to prophet) accountability, but he admits that it is difficult to get prophets to voluntarily submit their messages to scrutiny.

But Keith Hazel, a prophet from Calgary, Alberta, and the leader of Life-Links, a fellowship of sixty churches, says efforts at peer accountability within the prophetic movement are often ineffective.

"Most are accountable to each other, and no one ever calls them to give explanation to their unfulfilled and often dramatic prophetic words," he says. "There is a tendency to speak esoterically about mysterious and undefined things and later reinterpret them to prove that they are indeed true prophets."

Hazel suggests that the current prophetic movement has been diverted with the advancement of personal agendas and the building of reputations to comply with an "American superstar brand of Christianity." "In the context of the New Testament, this is unique," he contends, "since the prophets of the Bible loved obscurity and went about their work with humility."

Wagner agrees that the movement has its share of mavericks. But in his view, the issue is maturity, not heresy. "Where are we now when it comes to having a functional accountability system?" he asks. "On a scale of one to ten, we're at about a four. Prophets tend to be independent, so they're not under the direct covering of an apostle. Most prophets are hypersensitive to criticism. But it's a function of insecurity, because we're in the beginning of a movement."

While some may have a perception of prophets ministering in independence, many note a trend toward partnership and cooperation of prophets with other ministries in the church. "We're seeing prophetic ministry becoming integrated into a place of safety and balance by prophets' willingness to function alongside other seasoned ministries for accountability," Clem Ferris says. "The most seasoned and trustworthy prophetic voices today will demonstrate a spirit of submission, humility, and love while walking with fellow local church elders."

Michael Fletcher notes that the network of churches he oversees ultimately owes its effectiveness to the ministry of prophets who partner with other ministries in their midst. "They are the edge; they help us stay ahead of our game," he says. "Prophets provoke in the local church the reality of God; they enable us to find where people best fit in the body; they provoke the use of spiritual gifts in others."

ABOUT THE AUTHOR

Matthew D. Green served for four years as editor of *Ministry Today* magazine. He is currently a freelance writer and director of communications for Pioneers, a mission agency supporting more than one hundred eighty church-planting teams among unreached people groups in eighty-two countries. His Web site may be found at www.matthewdgreen.com.

FOR FURTHER STUDY

Bill Hamon, *Apostles, Prophets and the Coming Moves of God*

Cindy Jacobs, *The Voice of God: How God Speaks Personally and Corporately to His Children Today*

C. Peter Wagner, editor, *Pastors & Prophets: Protocol for Healthy Churches*

Mike Bickle, *Growing in the Prophetic*

CHAPTER 6

A Voice to the Nations

—CINDY JACOBS

SUMMARY

Beyond the realm of church pews and prayer meetings, God is using prophetic messages to transform nations and demonstrate His power on a global level.

SEVERAL YEARS AGO I spoke at a stadium event in Costa Rica. We were launching a massive prayer movement for Central America. After leaving the platform, I noticed a man sitting at the side who had obviously had a stroke of some kind. I knew that he had come for the prayer event and that he must be a man of influence in the nation, but I did not know anything else about him. As I walked past where he was sitting, I received a small nudge to go back and tell him that he would be the next president of the country. I immediately dismissed that thought and kept walking.

A moment later, I once again felt that I should turn around and go tell the man that he would be the next president. Right away, I shot back with a response, "There is no way that I am going to prophesy that man is going to be president! He looks so sick that he could die at any moment!"

Still walking, this time the voice that I know so well said to me, "Cindy Jacobs, you turn around and go tell that man that it is My will for him to be the next president of this country!" My friend, have you ever had your mother call you to do something by using both of your names? In my household that meant I was going to be in big trouble if I didn't do what my parents were telling me to. At that point I feared God more than what people might say if I missed hearing correctly. I whipped around on my heel and went back to the person God was so interested in speaking to.

Looking in the kind eyes of the man who I later found out was Don Abel Pacheco, I prophesied, "The Lord says that if you remain humble, you will be the next president of Costa Rica, and God will use you to expose corruption in this land."

Two years later my husband, Mike, and I went back to speak at a conference sponsored by Enlace in Costa Rica. Before we left, we received a phone call from our friends, and they said, "The president of Costa Rica would like to meet with you." We queried, "Who is the president?" They replied, "Don Abel Pacheco, the man you prophesied would be the next president."

Upon our arrival for our meeting with the president, he put out his hand and smiled and said, "Well, you were right, I am the president. What is the next thing that God says for my nation?" We were amazed to see him strong and healed.

The Lord has used President Pacheco to expose corruption and turn around the economy of the nation. During our meeting he smiled and said, "I never had thought about running for president until I received that prophecy. I did not want to be like Jonah in the belly of the whale, and so I obeyed God."

This chapter is going to deal with the unusual issue of God using prophets and prophetic people to transform nations. Perhaps most people will not actually prophesy over the future president of a nation, but many will be used of God to speak prophetically to people in their circle of influence who will change their neighborhoods, cities, and nations.

Over the past several years many people in the body of Christ have become familiar with the gift of prophecy. This is good, because 1 Corinthians 14:1 encourages us, "Pursue love, and desire spiritual gifts, but especially that you may prophesy." Of all the gifts of the Holy Spirit we are to especially desire to prophesy.

During the 1980s there was a special emphasis on personal prophecy. In the new century, God is highlighting the work of the prophet, which we see listed in the Ephesians 4:11–12 passage: "And He Himself gave some to be apostles, some prophets, some evangelists, and some pastors and teachers, for the equipping of the saints for the work of ministry, for the edifying of the body of Christ."

Bill Hamon, founder of Christian International and one of the fathers of the modern-day prophetic movement, has been used of God many times to prophesy to nations. One of the most dramatic examples of a prophetic word helping to change a nation was given through Bishop Hamon during the time of apartheid in South Africa in 1996.

During that time many were saying that the only way to end apartheid was through a bloody revolution. Some were saying that blood was going to run in the streets, and fear was running high in the nation. In the midst of this, Hamon prophesied to the churches that—if they would pray—there would be no bloody revolution, but a bloodless transition. History tells us that the churches did, indeed, pray, and the revolution was miraculously bloodless.

There are times that God will even use a prophet to reveal His will to a nonbelieving ruler. Take the case of Cyrus. God in His omniscience foresaw and spoke through His servant Isaiah around a hundred years before the birth of Cyrus that he would rebuild the temple in Jerusalem. Since Cyrus was a contemporary of the prophet Daniel and reigned over the kingdom where Daniel was an official, it is not too far-fetched to think that it was Daniel himself whom God used to show Cyrus the prophecy given by Isaiah.

> Many will be used of God to speak prophetically to people in their circle of influence who will change their neighborhoods, cities, and nations.

God used Cyrus to help fulfill the word of the Lord spoken by the prophet Jeremiah that the Israelites would come out of exile in Babylon after seventy years. Cyrus was so touched to find his name in a prophecy given through the court prophet, Isaiah, that he proclaimed in Ezra 1:2: "Thus says Cyrus king of Persia: All the kingdoms of the earth the LORD God of heaven has given me. And He has commanded me to build Him a house in Jerusalem which is in Judah."

I believe that one of the functions of the office of the prophet that we are seeing restored today is prophesying to nations. God gave me a prophecy along this line, which I delivered at the Apostolic Council of Prophetic Elders meeting in 2000: "For the Lord says that I am getting ready to put a prophet with a mayor and a prophet with a governor and a prophet with a president. There is a season coming in which I will connect my prophets with the presidents and kings of this world."

Since that day we are hearing reports of numbers of prophets who are having personal meetings with presidents and giving them the word of the Lord. While having dinner at a friend's home in Colorado Springs, the Lord suddenly gave me a prophecy for the African nation of Benin. It actually came during a word I was giving to our friend, Gunnar Olson. Gunnar is the founder of the International Christian Chamber of Commerce and had been working with the president of Benin for some time.

The story of this Christian president is an interesting one, because God used a prophetic dream given to a pastor in a strong way to help bring him to the Lord. Many years ago a brother named Pastor Romain Zannou was awakened in the night by a dream in which God spoke to him to go and witness to the then Marxist dictator Matthieu Kerekou. The pastor did not want to go, as Kerekou had the reputation of being a violent man, and the pastor knew that he did not like Christians. However, the Lord urged the pastor over and over to go. Finally, Pastor Romaine went, with much fear and trepidation.

In those days, in order to get an audience with the dictator, you went and sat in a big room and asked for an audience. Romaine went and was surprised when he was called in to meet with the leader. Trembling, the pastor told Kerekou why he had come and how the Lord had given him a dream telling him to go and tell Kerekou that he needed to be born again. This led to a number of dialogues between the two and ended with the pastor getting tossed out and told not to return.

However, by this time, Pastor Romaine knew that he had a mandate from the Lord to win the leader to Christ. Every day for eighteen months, which included both the rainy season and the long, hot, dry season, he went and sat and waited for an audience. Finally, after the long wait, the leader invited him in once again and gave his heart to the Lord.

Little did I know when I gave the prophecy to Gunnar that he would take it and place it in the hands of Kerekou, who was now the president of Benin. The president was so touched by the prophecy, which spoke of the mighty way God wanted to use this country that had been built upon and dedicated to voodoo, that he read the word of the Lord to his cabinet. He also read it to parliament and over the radio. Before he read the prophecy, he stated, "This is what the Lord says to our nation." Benin is a nation destined to change other nations in a region where war has raged.

I was interested to find that throughout the Old Testament, different government leaders officially appointed prophets. King David had Gad, who was called a *chozeh* or seer (1 Chron. 21:9), as well as Nathan, who was called a *nabiy* (2 Sam. 12:1). According to *Fausset's Bible Dictionary*, the seer beheld the visions of God and the prophet proclaimed the divine truth revealed to David as one of the official order in a more direct way.

Solomon had Iddo the seer (2 Chron. 9:29), and Jehu was a seer under Jehoshaphat (2 Chron. 20:34). Isaiah was a prophet during the time of King Uzziah, and some think that he was a royal relation. Aaron was a prophet to Moses, and Fausset says that prophets superceded, reproved, encouraged, set up, or put down kings—as Elisha did in Jehu's case. Deborah was both a government leader (a judge) and a prophet. Daniel was a prophet and government official under at least three, possibly four, administrations.

God has used His prophets to bring righteousness and justice through prophetic declarations numbers of times in history. One of the more recent occurrences took place in July 2004 when *Charisma* editor J. Lee Grady was in Guatemala. While ministering, Lee felt led of the Lord to declare that the *machismo* spirit over Guatemala was to come down. At that time Guatemala had the highest murder rate of women in all of Central America. One week after this declaration, the government of the nation addressed the issue of violence and put in a commission to study the problem of violence against women.

> God has used His prophets to bring righteousness and justice through prophetic declarations numbers of times in history.

There are some prophets who not only prophesy concerning nations and changes to nations, but they are also Issachar prophets. My friend Chuck Pierce is one of these. He not only prophesies about nations, but he also gives specific time frames in which the things he prophesies will take place.

For instance, during the Iraq War, all the troops were on the lookout for Saddam Hussein. Chuck was in a meeting one night in San Antonio, Texas, when God spoke to him in the middle of our friend Dutch Sheets's teaching. (Dutch and Chuck often flow together in the midst of their teachings with a time of prayer or a prophetic word.)

Chuck jumped up and said, "God has shown me that if we pray right now, Saddam Hussein will be captured this week." The whole conference erupted in intercession, which included prophetic declarations from some military leaders. True to the word of the Lord, Saddam was captured by the end of the week.

One of the major reasons that prophets speak to nations is to encourage God's people to respond to the word of the Lord. It is not God's will for judgment and devastation to come to nations. He often will speak to a prophet to give a warning to avert judgment and call His people to pray. (See 2 Chronicles 7:14; Amos 3:7.)

A few years ago the Lord spoke a very dire prophecy to me concerning Argentina. Because I have ministered many years in that nation, I asked a group of large church pastors and leaders if they would meet with me to judge the word. The Lord told me that the economy of the nation was going to collapse and that the streets of Buenos Aires were going to be filled with violence and rioting.

While they did not reject the word, this was hard to swallow, because Buenos Aires has always been such a civilized city. Nevertheless, the economy did collapse. However, a great move of prayer and unity has taken place in the nation since that time, and Christian leaders are beseeching God for the nation. I know that God is going to heal Argentina and once again raise it up as a leader of nations.

At times God will also give a prophecy to a nation so that the people will rise up in faith and believe God for mighty things to transpire. This has happened to me, and I have been amazed to see how a prophecy given to a nation will catalyze a whole country to believe the Lord for a powerful move of God. One of the most powerful examples of this that I know of in my own prophetic ministry has been that which was given for the Philippines.

The prophecy was first given during a conference sponsored by Harvest International Ministries in California, and it concerned Jerome Ocampo, the leader of the Jesus Revolution Youth movement of the Philippines. While prophesying over him, the word of the Lord suddenly came up for the nation. There were many points to the prophesy, but several of them have already transpired:

- Oil would be discovered in the ocean off the Philippines. Since then, a rich deposit of oil has been found.

- The Lord was going to cause the supreme court of the land to take from the rich to give to the poor. Without my knowing, the Supreme Court of the Philippines had been considering a case for some time concerning money that had been taken from poor coconut farmers. The court ruled that the money should be given back to the workers.

- There would be revival among the young military officers. Since that time there has been a military uprising of young officers in their mid-twenties to protest corruption in the government. There has also been a move of God among the military leaders.

The prophetic word is transformational when God's people believe it. Second Chronicles 20:20 says, "Believe in the LORD your God, and you shall be established; believe His prophets, and you shall prosper."

Here are some major points of how God uses prophets in the transformation of a nation:

1. To release hope and faith
2. To give direction
3. To reprove and correct
4. To release warnings of judgment and the call to pray
5. To help prophesy structure
6. To declare God's will into a region
7. To transition nations into God's destiny
8. To anoint leaders to serve in government

When Jesus ascended, He left gifts in the earth to fill all things. (See Ephesians 4:10.) It stands to reason that all things (structures such as government, education, politics, art, drama, and other societal institutions) will not be filled with all Christ designed for them without these gifts in operation. This particularly is true for nations. Prophets are God's voice used to expose, shift, and bring transition to nations.

ABOUT THE AUTHOR

Cindy Jacobs is cofounder, with her husband, Mike, of Generals of Intercession, based in Colorado Springs (www.generals.org). She is the author of numerous books, including *The Voice of God*.

FOR FURTHER STUDY

Bill Hamon, *Apostles, Prophets, and the Coming Moves of God*

Bill Hamon, *Prophets and the Prophetic Movement, Vol. 2: God's Prophetic Move Today*

Francis Frangipane, *Discerning of Spirits*

Cindy Jacobs, *The Voice of God*

CHAPTER 7

2000 Years of Prophecy

—Vinson Synan

SUMMARY

They've been persecuted, celebrated, and ignored—but the church owes its expansion in many sectors to the voice of its prophets.

ALTHOUGH SOME SEE recent prophetic movements as a new phenomenon in church history, there is a rich tradition of prophetic ministry that goes back for thousands of years.

In biblical times, both the Old and New Testaments gave prominence to the office of prophet and the ministry of prophecy. Most of the Old Testament scriptures were given to us by the major and minor prophets who spoke the words of the Lord to their own and future generations.

In the New Testament, the office of prophet was held in high esteem, since the church was built on the foundation of the apostles and prophets. (See Ephesians 2:20.) In addition, there are many references to prophets and prophecy and even an entire book devoted to it: the Book of Revelation.

A brief survey of church history indicates that the ministry of prophets has engendered controversy at best and outright persecution at worst. However, there is no indication that these offices and ministries were ever withdrawn from the church, but that they would continue until the "perfect" comes at the return of Christ. (See 1 Corinthians 13:8–12.)

CENTURIES OF SUPPRESSION

Indeed, the records of the first generations after the Resurrection show that there were many prophets still active in the church. The numbers, however, gradually decreased as the church developed more highly organized structures under the care of local bishops. As time went on, those who claimed to be "apostles" and "prophets" were reduced to wander as traveling itinerants who were not often welcomed by the bishops.

In the *Didache*, a document written in the second century, rules were enforced to control the prophets who traveled from diocese to diocese trying to find a place to minister. They were always to be welcomed at first and then closely watched thereafter.

Some of the rules stated that if a prophet stayed more than three days in one place, he would be seen as a "false prophet." Furthermore, if he took an offering or prophesied that a meal should be served, or if he failed to practice what he taught, he also would be exiled as a false prophet.

Indeed, in that period prophets were seen as little more than wandering medicine men. With these obstacles, prophecy began to die out in the church as bishops became more entrenched in their hierarchical offices and home territories.

In the third century, there was an attempt to revive prophecy to the same level that had been seen in the days of the New Testament church. The second-century followers of a Charismatic movement led by Montanus prophesied and spoke in ecstatic tongues about the Second Coming of Christ.

They also claimed that their prophecies should be accepted as being equal to the canon of the New Testament and held that further revelations were still being given to the church. In the end, rightly or wrongly, the church rejected Montanism along with the prophecies that were produced by the movement.

For long periods of time, the voice of the prophet was seldom heard in Christian lands. In the Roman Catholic Church, prophecy was reduced mostly to foretelling future events. Famous Catholic prophecies by such figures as St. Edward the Confessor, St. Malachy, and St. John of the Cross were held in awe because they predicted future events related to the papacy and the fate of the Catholic Church.

The most famous Catholic prophet and predictor of future events was Nostradamus, a sixteenth-century physician and mystic from southern France. His arcane and exotic prophecies are still the subject of intense fascination to this day.

In the Protestant world, Martin Luther and John Calvin had little use for prophecies and other charismatic gifts, since they felt that all revealed truth was finally captured in the sacred Scriptures. Luther never tired of railing against the "swarming" prophets and "babbling" tongues speakers of his day. They were all "false prophets" and dangerous enemies of the Reformation. During the Peasants War, Luther recommended that such people be drawn and quartered.

Indeed, the Anabaptist "prophets" in the German city of Muenster were massacred by leaders of the Reformation. Despite these circumstances, Lutherans in later centuries experienced prophecies in the various Pietist and Charismatic movements that occasionally arose in Lutheran domains.

> There is no indication that these offices and ministries were ever withdrawn from the church, but that they would continue until the "perfect" comes at the return of Christ.

In time, the reformed followers of John Calvin went on to develop a view of the gifts and ministries of the Holy Spirit called "cessationism." This view held that the miraculous gifts and ministries of the apostolic age ceased with the apostles, and the church needed only the Scriptures and the sacraments for salvation. Despite this trend, various sons of the Reformed tradition, such as Jonathan Edwards and the later Charismatics, experienced great revivals and prophetic manifestations.

For several centuries, therefore, the office of prophet and the proclamation of prophetic messages were vigorously opposed and persecuted by both Protestants and Catholics. Around 1700, a prophetic movement arose among the Protestant Huguenots in France. Because they were given to many prophecies, they earned the name "the prophets of Cevennes."

In time, the French Catholic Church rejected the movement, and many of the prophets were martyred for their faith. Some of them escaped to England where they were known as the French Prophets. There they influenced John Wesley himself.

It was only in the nineteenth century that tongues and prophecy again appeared prominently in the church. In the 1830s in Britain, a group of aristocratic Anglicans and Presbyterians revived prophecy under the leadership of Edward Irving and John Nelson Darby and also attempted to restore the office of apostle to the church. After a degree of rejection by both Anglican and Presbyterian authorities, the group organized the independent Catholic Apostolic Church, where thousands of prophecies not only were uttered but also were written down for the faithful to read.

Their basic premise was that the fivefold ministry must be restored to the church before Christ could return. Their prophecies, however, did not foresee the ultimate failure of the movement. By 1900, most of the churches had disbanded in England, although a vigorous church continued in Germany.

CHARISMATIC/PENTECOSTAL RENEWAL

With the advent of modern Pentecostalism, the gift of prophecy exploded again among Christians who received the baptism in the Holy Spirit accompanied by the gift of tongues. The earliest Pentecostals were sure that all of the gifts of the Spirit were being restored to the church, including the gift of prophecy.

Although tongues received most of the attention, Pentecostals soon began to see tongues and interpretation as being equal to prophecy (based on 1 Corinthians 14:5). Many cases of tongues, with the attendant interpretations, became directive prophecies for the thousands of missionaries and evangelists who went to the far corners of the earth in the wake of the Azusa Street revival.

When William J. Seymour sent his followers forth, they usually went with a personal prophecy from Seymour. Several major Pentecostal missions thrusts came as a result of these and other prophecies.

For instance, the Pentecostal revival in Chile came partly as a result of a prophecy given by a poor night watchman to the pastor of the Valparaiso Methodist Church, W. C. Hoover. The prophecy called on the most spiritual members of the church to pray each day at the 5:00 p.m. teatime. "I intend to baptize you with tongues of fire" was the burden of the prophecy. In 1909 a monumental revival broke out in the church with many cases of prophecies, dreams, visions, and speaking in tongues.

After the Methodist authorities rejected the revival in a trial proceeding in September 1909, Hoover and thirty-seven Chilean former Methodists organized the Pentecostal Methodist Church. Today the latest government census credits the Pentecostal Methodist Church with having two and one-half million members in Chile.

In 1910 in South Bend, Indiana, a prophecy was given to Daniel Berg and Gunnar Vingren in a prayer meeting, calling on them to go somewhere in the world called "Para." After consulting an atlas of the world in a Chicago public library, they found the state of Para in northeastern Brazil.

Without questioning they found their way to Belen on the Para River in 1910, and in 1912, they organized the first church movement to use the name *Assemblies of God* (AG) out of a local Baptist church. By the end of the century the Brazilian AG church numbered more than fifteen million members. Together with other Pentecostal and Charismatic groups, Pentecostal renewalists in Brazil now number some seventy-nine million persons.

In New York City, a prophecy was given to Ivan Voronaev in Manhattan in 1919. The words of the prophecy said, "Voronaev, Voronaev, journey to Russia." A recent convert to Pentecostalism from a Russian Baptist church, Voronaev took his family to Ukraine in 1920. During his ministry, more than three hundred fifty Pentecostal churches were planted in many Slavic nations.

In 1943, Voronaev was martyred in a communist prison, but the movements he founded are now exploding across the Slavic world, the largest of which is in Ukraine, a nation that now boasts emerging megachurches in many cities.

In Johannesburg, South Africa, in 1936, an illiterate English evangelist Smith Wigglesworth prophesied to David du Plessis, calling him to leave the "Jerusalem" of his native South Africa. The prophecy told of a worldwide ministry of traveling to introduce Pentecost to the mainline churches.

In what is now seen as predictive of the Charismatic Renewal, Wigglesworth's utterance spoke of a mighty Pentecostal outpouring in the mainline churches that would make the older Pentecostal movement "look like a joke" in comparison.

Du Plessis became a world ambassador for Pentecostalism, and, indeed, a mighty Charismatic movement in the mainline churches broke out in 1960. In his last years, du Plessis was known as "Mr. Pentecost."

Oral Roberts, who brought the message of divine healing into the living rooms of the nation, received a prophecy in his home in Enid, Oklahoma, in 1948, which impelled him into a worldwide ministry.

While pastoring a small Pentecostal church in rural Oklahoma, Roberts heard a voice saying, "You will take My healing power to your generation." His subsequent healing ministry and Oral Roberts University attest to the power of the prophecy.

In Los Angeles, on the night of December 26, 1952, Demos Shakarian, troubled by the seeming failure of his layman's movement, was given an extended vision of the world with an army of Spirit-filled businessmen taking the gospel to the four corners of the earth.

His wife, Rose, prophesied that what he had seen in his vision would soon come to pass. The Full Gospel Business Men went on to be a major carrier of the Pentecostal/Charismatic revival in the next three decades, bringing millions of mainline Christians into the experience of the baptism in the Holy Spirit.

The advent of the Charismatic movement among Protestants in 1960 and Roman Catholics in 1967 opened the door for a new flood of prophetic utterances in the thousands of prayer meetings and conferences that mushroomed around the world in the 1970s and 1980s.

> In the Protestant world, Martin Luther and John Calvin had little use for prophecies and other charismatic gifts since they felt that all revealed truth was finally captured in the sacred Scriptures.

As a movement aimed at restoring all the gifts and ministries to the church, tongues, prophecies, healings, and exorcisms became major attractions of many Charismatic ministries. Whereas the older Pentecostals gave spontaneous and extemporaneous prophecies, many Charismatics, especially Catholic ones, carefully wrote out their prophecies and read them before large and expectant audiences.

The most famous prophecy of this period was given at the Kansas City (Missouri) Conference in 1977. There was weeping and repentance among the fifty thousand people gathered in Arrowhead Stadium as the words, "The body of My Son is broken," boomed over the speakers. A promise of ultimate victory brought cheers from the multitude in the stadium.

Although the gift of prophecy continued to be regularly exercised in countless Pentecostal and Charismatic gatherings around the world, new prophetic teachers arose in the 1980s and 1990s to draw further attention to the prophetic gift in the church.

One of these, Bill Hamon, led a movement that included mass individual directive prophecies in large gatherings. As people lined up, the prophets gave a personal prophecy to everyone in attendance, at times numbering hundreds of people. These prophecies put a strain on the prophets, since they were asked to produce prophecies to multitudes of perfect strangers. As a result, Hamon founded a school of the prophets in Florida where students came from near and far to learn how to exercise the gift.

ENCOURAGING THE GIFT

Recent prophecy movements have raised several serious questions among church leaders and theologians. For instance, some think that mass prophecy on demand often leads to mechanical and meaningless prophecies that could actually be harmful to the recipients. Usually people seeking prophetic guidance are counseled to seek confirmation elsewhere and not base any major decision on just one prophecy.

Additionally, the idea that a prophet could be wrong on a certain percentage of predictive prophecies and improve with practice has also been questioned by many, since the overwhelming tradition, especially in the Old Testament, is that false predictions are prima facie evidence of a false prophet. The practice of learning to prophesy in a classroom setting seems to take a gift of the Spirit, which is given and controlled by the Holy Spirit, and place it in human hands apart from a worshiping community.

Despite these and other questions, the church should be thankful that the gift of prophecy has been abundantly manifested in this generation. Thousands of mighty ministries have been energized by words of prophecy.

A recent example is the prophecy made many years ago that Reinhard Bonnke would one day see 1,000,000 souls converted in one service. This actually took place in his millennium crusade in Lagos, Nigeria, in 2000. On one night, 1,093,745 persons signed decision cards testifying to having accepted Christ as their Savior. May we have many more such prophecies and many more such results.

ABOUT THE AUTHOR

Vinson Synan, PhD, is professor of divinity and dean of the School of Divinity at Regent University. A respected church historian, Synan is the author of numerous books, including *The Century of the Holy Spirit.*

FOR FURTHER STUDY

Vinson Synan, *The Holiness-Pentecostal Tradition: Charismatic Movements in the Twentieth Century*

Donald W. Dayton, *Theological Roots of Pentecostalism*

CHAPTER 8

Putting Personal Prophecy to the Test

—EDDIE HYATT

SUMMARY

Don't quench it, but don't abuse it. Here are indispensable biblical guidelines for keeping personal prophecy on track.

IT SEEMS THAT almost everyone has an amusing or thought-provoking anecdote about an encounter with personal prophecy. For instance, a prophet once exhorted me that I no longer had to be concerned about my unsaved little brother. God had revealed to him, he said, that my little brother would be saved and there was no need for any concern. In private, I shared with this "prophet" that I had not been concerned about my little brother because I did not have a little brother. Obviously embarrassed, he replied, "I will have to be more careful." This experience highlighted for me the potential danger of personal prophecy gone awry.

An equal danger, however, is when the church reacts to such extremes and rejects or discourages personal prophecy altogether. Paul gives clear instructions in this regard: "Do not quench the Spirit," he says, and "do not despise prophecies" (1 Thess. 5:19–20). In verse 21 he then balances the former two verses by saying, "Test all things; hold fast what is good."

Paul's approach to prophecy may be described as "openness without naïveté and discernment without judgmentalism." He does not squelch their enthusiasm, but he presents guidelines that will help them derive the greatest benefit from the gift.

Throughout his letters, in Paul's instructions on prophecy, several key guidelines emerge that are particularly relevant to personal prophecy:

1. It is given as the Spirit wills.
2. It is given for confirming and encouraging.
3. It is given as a free gift of grace.
4. It is given to glorify Christ.

In 1 Corinthians 12:11, Paul clearly states that all the gifts—including prophecy—are not gifts that a person carries and operates in at his own will, but are manifestations that come forth as the Spirit wills.

Recently my wife, Susan, and I were in our van about to back out of our driveway when the Holy Spirit interrupted us. Sue was suddenly aware of an inner compassion flowing out to our next-door neighbor who was working in her yard. We had only recently moved into this house, and this neighbor, upon discovering that we were Christians, introduced herself as a backslidden preacher from Brooklyn, New York. We did not attempt to discuss our faith with her and in the succeeding days sought merely to be good neighbors.

On this day, with God's prompting, Sue called her by name—"Adele!" Upon hearing her name, Adele walked over to the side of our vehicle. Without a prior sense that it was coming, Sue broke forth with an utterance in tongues. I leaned across the seat and spoke the interpretation, which was a personal word of prophecy to Adele, "My daughter, you are precious in My sight." Adele burst into tears and then into praying in tongues. It was a powerful encounter, facilitated by a personal prophecy that came forth, not as we willed, but as the Spirit willed.

Contrary to the biblical model, some teach that believers can prophesy at their own volition or will. I heard one well-known prophet insist that, just as it took Pentecostals several decades to discover that they could speak or pray in tongues at will, many in the body of Christ are now discovering that they can prophesy at will.

Proponents of this teaching point to the fact that, in 1 Corinthians 14:15, Paul says, "I will pray with the spirit"—an obvious reference to praying in tongues. They give emphasis to the "I will" in this passage and reason that if one can will to pray or speak in tongues, then one can also will to prophesy.

This ignores the context of Paul's discussion. When Paul says, "I will pray with the spirit," he is referring to the private, devotional tongues in which he wills—or chooses—to pray. He distinguishes between private, devotional tongues in which he prays at will and the public manifestation of tongues that requires interpretation and comes forth as the Spirit wills—a very important distinction.

The idea that one can prophesy at will has resulted in many "prophets" operating out of their soul realm (mind, will, and emotions) rather than from the Spirit. I have observed prophets who have become very adept at "reading" people and then giving a word that the recipient could easily apply to his or her own situation.

> Prophetic ministry in the New Testament will thus confirm, strengthen, and reinforce, not mediate and legislate.

When this approach is coupled with immaturity or an unsavory character, it becomes extremely dangerous, with the prophet often prophesying to impress and manipulate others and to enhance his own standing. At this point, the prophet has crossed the dividing line from Christian prophecy, with its source in the Holy Spirit, to fortune-telling and psychic phenomena, with their sources in the human psyche and possibly the demonic.

In 1 Corinthians 14:3 Paul gives the primary purpose of prophecy in very clear and succinct terms: "But he who prophesies speaks edification and exhortation and comfort to men." In verse 31 he says that all may prophesy that all may be encouraged. On the other hand, Paul says in 2 Timothy 3:16 that Scripture is good for doctrine (teaching), for reproof (rebuke), for correction, and for instruction in righteousness.

When individuals begin to utilize personal prophecy for purposes reserved primarily for Scripture, it is time to beware. This distinction was made very real to me as the result of an erroneous prophecy that came forth in a congregation where I once pastored.

Near the close of a Sunday evening service, a woman, who was quite new to our assembly, brought forth a very severe rebuke to the congregation in the form of a prophecy. She spoke this word during a time of spontaneous worship as people were responding to a very real sense of God's love and presence. As she concluded her prophecy, I could see confusion appearing on people's faces, and I knew I must address what had just happened. I proceeded to inform the congregation that the word just spoken was not from

God and encouraged them to ignore what had been said and to continue worshiping.

After the service, this woman came to me very upset. I found myself pointing her to the two passages mentioned above and explaining to her the different purposes of prophecy and Scripture—prophecy being for confirming and encouraging, and Scripture being for teaching, rebuking, and correcting. I then offered her five minutes in our next service to present a rebuke to the congregation. "But don't prophesy to us," I said. "Take your Bible and show us where you think we are missing the mark."

"Oh, I could never do that," she replied.

"You just did it," I said, "but you hid behind a 'thus saith the Lord.'" The point is that we must not allow personal prophecy to usurp the place of Scripture, prayer, and the leading of the Holy Spirit in our lives.

In the Old Testament, people often went to the prophet, or seer, to obtain direction and insight. In the New Testament, however, there is not a single example of anyone seeking guidance from a prophet. In the New Testament, the indwelling Holy Spirit is the right and privilege of every believer, making the mediation of a special prophet unnecessary. Prophetic ministry in the New Testament will thus confirm, strengthen, and reinforce, not mediate and legislate.

At this point some will want to distinguish between the *gift* of prophecy and the *office* of the prophet. The New Testament, however, does not make such a fine distinction. In the New Testament, prophetic ministry is available—at least potentially—to all believers. (See 1 Corinthians 14:1, 5, 31, 39.)

Although some individuals are referred to as prophets, Pentecostal scholar Gordon D. Fee may well be correct when he notes in his commentary on 1 Corinthians that those called prophets in the New Testament are just as likely to be those who prophesied more frequently than others as those who bore an official title.[1]

In his first letter to the Corinthians, Paul refers to prophecy as a *charisma*, the Greek word that is translated "spiritual gift" in our English Bibles. *Charisma* and its plural form, *charismata*, are derived from *charis*, the Greek word for "grace." Prophecy, therefore, is literally a grace gift. It is given freely out of God's kindness and favor, not because of any merit in the one who prophesies. Paul uses *charisma*, no doubt, to undermine the egoism and pride of the Corinthians in the exercise of their spiritual gifts—including prophecy. Church history demonstrates that every generation needs to be reminded that these gifts flow out of God's grace and are not badges of spiritual superiority.

Although prophecy may offer hope and encouragement to individuals, the ultimate purpose is to draw them to Christ. Revelation 19:10 says, "For the essence of prophecy is to give a clear witness for Jesus" (NLT). This coincides with John 16:14 (NLT), where Jesus says that when the Holy Spirit comes, "He will bring me glory."

When prophecy becomes too anthropocentric (human-centered), there is cause for concern. When prophecy becomes earthbound and is used to enhance the status of a movement and its leaders, it has veered outside the biblical parameters. When prophecy is used to manipulate people to give money or to accept a new teaching, it has become pseudoprophecy. The Holy Spirit is in the earth to lift up Jesus, and true prophecy will redound to His glory.

To derive the greatest benefit from the prophetic gift, we must avoid the extremes of a too controlled or an uncontrolled prophetic ministry. A too controlled approach will quench the gift altogether, while an uncontrolled approach will inevitably lead to misuse, abuse, and disaster. Mature pastoral guidance that both values the prophetic gift and understands the potential pitfalls therein is indispensable. With an open and mature approach to personal prophecy, perhaps Paul's description of a genuine prophetic meeting in 1 Corinthians 14:24–25 can be realized in our own gatherings.

He says that when the unlearned or unbelievers come into a meeting where the prophetic gift is flowing freely, as they listen, their secret thoughts will be laid bare, and they will fall down on their knees and worship God, declaring, "God is really here among you." May leaders seek God's guidance in shepherding this powerful gift so that people both inside and outside the church may be challenged and edified through the gift of prophecy.

ABOUT THE AUTHOR

Eddie L. Hyatt, DMin, is the author of *2000 Years of Charismatic Christianity* and is the cofounder, with his wife, Susan, of Hyatt International Ministries, based in Fort Worth, Texas.

FOR FURTHER STUDY

Jack Deere, *The Beginner's Guide to the Gift of Prophecy*

Graham Cooke, *Developing Your Prophetic Gifting*

Frank Dimazio, *Developing the Prophetic Gifting*

CHAPTER 9

Can You Spot a Prophet?

—J. LEE GRADY

SUMMARY

In an age of cheap imitations, here's how to embrace genuine prophetic ministry—and reject the counterfeits.

CALL ME A reluctant prophet. I was a shy child and an insecure teenager, yet God called me to speak for Him. I don't have a polished preaching style, and I hate to hear my voice on tape. But God called me to prophesy in answer to a prayer I uttered when I was eighteen. I had read 1 Corinthians 14:1 (AMP), which says we should "earnestly desire" to prophesy.

So I told the Lord that if He needed me to speak for Him, I would. It was one of those "Here I am, Lord, send me" moments. I tried to place conditions on my availability. "I'll speak for You," I told God, "but (1) I'd rather write than speak since I don't like crowds; (2) I don't want to confront controversial subjects; and (3) I never intend to call someone out of an audience and give them a word from the Lord."

You can predict what happened. After serving behind the scenes for years as a writer and editor, I began to receive speaking invitations. Conference organizers wanted me to address controversial subjects in front of large audiences. And in the year 2000, I was tricked into giving personal prophecies to people

I didn't know. It happened in southern China during a visit with leaders of the underground church.

One of their leaders asked me to come to a meeting room in her hotel, and when I arrived there were fourteen other leaders waiting. "Brother Lee, we would like you to pray over each one of these people and prophesy to them," the woman said through a translator. Then she closed the door, knelt, and closed her eyes. I swallowed hard and breathed a prayer of surrender. An hour and a half later, everyone in the room had received a personal prophecy, and some were crying because they had been so encouraged.

Since that moment the Lord has used me to speak prophetically in many situations. I've called out people from audiences, offered prophetic direction to leaders, and, with great reluctance, given private words of correction. Most often the words I give others provide confirmation and encouragement. The messages are not spooky or weird. On the contrary, these words rekindle weak faith and remind the hearers that God's promised answers are on the way.

> It is dangerous for any prophet to come to a platform before his pride has been dismantled.

I don't like the prophet label, and I don't use it as a title. But I do believe that in this hour we desperately need the gift of prophecy in full operation. It is one of the most powerful weapons in the church's spiritual arsenal, yet it is the most misunderstood. It is also the most misused. Many people who have been wounded by the abuses of prophecy are tempted to throw the gift out altogether. No wonder the apostle Paul told the Thessalonians: "Do not despise prophecies" (1 Thess. 5:20). As much as the gift has been abused, we are not allowed to put it on the shelf.

How can we restore the value of this gift and safeguard our churches from its exploitation? I believe we must raise the standard for all those who claim to be prophets. In my study of prophets in the Bible, I've identified eight key qualities that distinguish true prophets from pretenders. We should expect these qualities to be evident in men and women who claim to speak for God today.

1. A true prophet clings to the Bible.

It may seem unnecessary to say this, but in today's spiritual climate we must. True prophets don't contradict, negate, or twist Scripture. Even if a prophet displays amazing anointing for miracles or accurate predictions, he should never be given a platform if the Word of God is not his final authority.

One of my favorite prophets in the Old Testament is Huldah. (See 2 Kings 22:1–20.) Although the entire nation of Judah was backslidden, this woman held fast to the Lord. When King Josiah learned that the scroll of Moses had been discovered, he sought out Huldah's counsel. We don't know much about her, but it is obvious that Huldah kept the fire of true worship burning. She remained a woman of the Word when the Bible was collecting cobwebs in a closet.

And when Huldah opened her mouth, fire came out. She spoke with the same commanding authority as her contemporary, Jeremiah. She pronounced God's judgment on Judah (a prophecy that quickly came to pass), and she gave a personal prophecy to Josiah, which was fulfilled as well. So it must be for all true prophets. They do not neglect the Word of God, even when society becomes decadent and religious leaders entertain compromise.

2. A true prophet's words will be confirmed by the Lord.

It was said in 1 Samuel 3:19–20 that none of Samuel's words fell to the ground. He was 100 percent accurate. He never missed it, and God backed up his message.

So what do we do when someone makes an inaccurate prophetic prediction? A genuine Christian who makes a mistake in prophecy should not be labeled a false prophet. But if prophets claim to speak for God, they must submit to correction and make apologies. Prophets who aren't willing to be corrected should not be in public ministry. Sometimes leaders in the body of Christ make embarrassing prophetic blunders because they are operating outside of their gifts. They may be called to be apostles or pastors, but they make impetuous prophetic declarations out of ignorance. They could avoid this error by staying inside the boundaries of their spiritual callings.

These people usually don't have evil motives, but the truth is that they are not gifted in the prophetic realm—and their mistakes bring dishonor to the Lord. Because of spiritual immaturity, we all have the potential of prophesying out of turn. We must assume responsibility for any idle words we speak.

3. A true prophet is fearless.

Few prophets in the Bible were graced with natural speaking ability. Moses stuttered, Esther was timid, and Jeremiah felt inadequate because of his youth. But God required them to overcome fear and self-consciousness.

The prophetess Deborah is a model of boldness. (See Judges 4:4–16.) She called Israel to war at a time when the nation was outnumbered by the Canaanites at least ten to one. Even her military commander, Barak, seemed unsure of victory—yet Deborah knew God would defeat His enemies supernaturally. She could face the battle with valiance because she knew what the outcome would be. Even though only a few tribes in Israel responded to her rallying cry, she did not allow the apathy of the people to dampen her zeal. A fierceness of spirit drove her to conquer.

A true prophet will not back down from what God has said, even if everyone else loses heart. The opinions or fears of men will not sway him, and his fire will not be dampened even when the church dismisses his message with yawns or criticism.

4. A true prophet is tested by the Lord in obscurity.

Ever notice that many prophets in the Bible emerged from nowhere? Elijah, for example, came from the backside of the desert to confront wicked King Ahab. (See 1 Kings 17:1–7.) Elijah went through a season of testing and preparation, but that process is hidden from us. True prophets will go through periods of hiddenness and intense brokenness. God must deal with pride, self-centeredness, and greed. The prophet must also learn to live in a place of intimate fellowship with God where the praises of men don't affect him.

> Prophecy is one of the most powerful weapons in the church's spiritual arsenal, yet it is the most misunderstood. It is also the most misused.

We should be wary of prophets who haven't spent time in the wilderness. It is dangerous for any prophet to come to a platform before his pride has been dismantled. True prophets also must be willing to remain nameless. Often they must stay behind the scenes and under the radar.

There are many nameless prophets in the Bible. One who is simply referred to as "a man of God" in 1 Kings 13:1 prophesied that Josiah would make sweeping spiritual reforms. This prophet's words were powerfully confirmed when the altar in the temple split open while King Jeroboam watched (v. 5). Yet this prophet—as anointed as he was—was tested by another unnamed prophet (who is simply called "an old prophet" in v. 11). Because the younger prophet had a streak of unyielded pride, he ended up dead (vv. 21–24). His story is a powerful reminder that anointing alone, without tested character, is not enough to sustain a messenger of God.

5. A true prophet can't be bought.

After Elisha healed Naaman, the prophet was offered several nice gifts (2 Kings 5:15–16). Elisha refused the rewards because he did not minister to Naaman for personal gain. Elisha would not allow an honorarium to become a stumbling block! Yet Elisha's assistant, Gehazi, went back to Naaman and cunningly suggested that his master would take some silver and clothes (vv. 20–22). Gehazi thought he could get away with deception, but the story ended in tragedy when Elisha found out. Gehazi became a leper as a result of his greed (v. 27).

Gehazi's leprosy is still spreading today. A spirit of merchandising has invaded the church, even among those who call themselves prophets. I once heard a prominent minister tell a church audience in Florida that he would give personal prophecies to anyone who would give $1,000 in the offering! (Amazingly, several people contributed.) If a man claims to speak for God, yet his motive is personal enrichment, he is inviting the same judgment that befell Ananias and Sapphira. (See Acts 5.) Such blatant charlatanism brings strange fire into the house of God. We shouldn't tolerate it.

6. A true prophet can't be compromised by power.

The prophet Nathan served King David as his adviser and was most likely on the palace payroll. Yet when it came time to confront David's adultery (and the murderous cover-up of his affair), Nathan did not hold back his rebuke. (See 2 Samuel 12:1–15.) He was not a yes man. Even though he risked losing his royal position, he was faithful to confront. Sometimes prophets will find themselves in cozy places. They may be tempted to look the other way when a church leader is in sin—especially if the pastor promises to invite the prophet back on a regular basis to receive a nice cash offering (otherwise known as a bribe).

Once I was invited to a conference in Idaho. When I arrived I could sense that the leadership of the ministry was in chaos. I prayed and felt the Lord told me to confront the leaders about an independent spirit. The Lord even gave me a warning that He would bring swift correction. The day I returned from the conference I learned that police in another state wanted the leader of the ministry because he owed back child support. This man was a rebel, and no one at the conference knew it but God. I could have withheld correction and perhaps maintained favor (and received an honorarium) from this ministry. But the important thing was to speak what God sent me to say.

7. A true prophet passes through God's fire.

Isaiah is one of the most oft-quoted prophets. Jesus often recited passages from his recorded prophecies. But Isaiah had to pay a price to speak such anointed words. He spent time in the fire of God's holiness.

A true prophet will submit when God places a hot coal on his lips. (See Isaiah 6:1–8.) If we expect the Lord to use our mouths, then we will have to embrace the process of sanctification—and it will involve purifying our speech as well as the motives from which we prophesy. A true prophet cannot speak for God and then use his mouth to criticize and destroy other people. A true prophet cannot preach about the mysteries of God and then use his tongue to curse or spread discord. A true prophet cannot call God's people to holiness one day and then engage in adultery or perversion the next. We must submit to the Holy Spirit's flame.

8. A true prophet has compassion.

We often think of Jeremiah as being harsh because he denounced Israel's sin and predicted judgment. But if we read between the lines we will realize that Jeremiah did not speak in an angry tone. Although he certainly felt the righteous anger of the Lord at times, he was usually weeping when he called Israel to repentance. When the wayward Israelites rejected Jeremiah's warning and decided to return to Egypt, the prophet followed them all the way to Egypt—urging them to turn back. Scholars believe that the prophet died in Egypt. Not only did he deliver a message to some stubborn people, but also his life was a living testimony of God's unfailing love to those who choose to reject Him.

Judgmental prophets are a dime a dozen. We need prophets today who will convey God's heart like Jeremiah. His constant weeping led him to say, "Oh, that my head were waters, and my eyes a fountain of tears" (Jer. 9:1). It's one thing to prophesy the right words. It's an entirely different thing to prophesy those words with God's tone of voice. Mature prophets will reflect God's tender emotions at the same time they deliver their message accurately.

ABOUT THE AUTHOR

J. Lee Grady is the editor of *Charisma* magazine and author of several books, including *10 Lies the Church Tells Women*. He has been an ordained minister in the International Pentecostal Holiness Church since 2000. He lives in the Orlando, Florida, area with his wife and four daughters.

FOR FURTHER STUDY

Cindy Jacobs, *The Voice of God*

Bill Hamon, *Prophets and Personal Prophecy*

CHAPTER 10

Speaking God's Thoughts

—ERNEST GENTILE

SUMMARY

Learn how to discern the still, small, prophetic voice of God in your life—and act on His direction.

IN RECENT YEARS, prophecy has become a topic of great interest among Bible-believing Christians—and rightly so. As people have been filled with the Holy Spirit and exposed to the charismatic gifts mentioned in the New Testament, the hunger to understand—and personally participate in—these gifts has increased dramatically.

Prophecy is most significant. Consider, for instance, the eight lists of spiritual gifts recounted in the New Testament. (See 1 Corinthians 12:8–10, 28–30; 13:1–3; 14:26; Romans 12:6–8; Ephesians 4:11; 1 Peter 4:10–11). Only one gift of the twenty mentioned is included in all eight lists: prophecy. Paul says, "Pursue love, and desire spiritual gifts, but especially that you may prophesy" (1 Cor. 14:1).

Charismatic leaders emphasize that prophecy is the superior gift God uses to edify (upbuild) the church. Consider three statements:

- In his book *The Era of the Spirit*, J. Rodman Williams says, "As far as the upbuilding of the fellowship is concerned, prophecy stands out as the most significant of all the Spirit's operations."[1]

- In his book *Prophets and Personal Prophecy*, Bill Hamon comments, "Prophecy stands out as the most significant of all the Spirit's operations."[2]

- Wayne Grudem points out in *The Gift of Prophecy in the New Testament Church and Today*, "Prophecy...is superior to the other gifts because the revelation on which it depends allows it to be suited to the specific needs of the moment, needs which may only be known to God."[3]

WHAT IS PROPHECY?

The root meaning of the Greek word *prophetein* is "to speak forth" (*pro* = "forth"; *phemi* = "to speak"). The King James Version consistently and correctly translates this verb as "to prophesy," not "to teach" or "preach." The early church realized that this "speaking forth" was more than a previously prepared sermon—it was an immediate message of God to His people through a divinely anointed utterance.

> Prophecy is God sharing *some* of His *innumerable* thoughts, and He graciously uses human messengers to do so; however, even a gifted prophet receives only a portion of the many good thoughts that God has available.

Prophecy became more understandable to me one day while lounging with my family on the sunny Pajaro Dunes Beach in California. While sitting on the sand, I noticed some grains had stuck to my moist hand. A foolish thought prodded me to count them. Immediately I realized how impossible it would be!

Psalm 139:17–18 suddenly came to mind: "How precious to me are your thoughts, O God! How vast is the sum of them! Were I to count them, they would outnumber the grains of sand. When I awake, I am still with you" (NIV) (or, "you are still thinking of me!" [TLB]). His thoughts toward *me* are more numerous than all the grains of sand on all the seashores of the earth!

Prophecy is God sharing *some* of His *innumerable* thoughts, and He graciously uses human messengers to do so; however, even a gifted prophet receives only a portion of the many good thoughts that God has available. The best that he or she can do is put the antenna of faith in a receptive mode, and then simply deliver the heavenly message received.

My definition of prophecy: "God shares His thoughts about a given situation by inspiring one of His Spirit-filled servants to speak these thoughts to the appropriate person or persons in understandable language and in the power of the Holy Spirit." As David Watson describes in *I Believe in the Church*, God enables His thoughts to be clearly verbalized through a Spirit-inspired person "to a particular person or group of persons, at a particular moment, for a particular purpose."[4]

PROPHECY IN THE EARLY CHURCH

As I wrote in *Your Sons and Daughters Shall Prophesy*: "The early church embraced an astounding belief.... They were convinced that the Jesus who had walked among humankind in a literal body now resided among them in the invisible Person of the Holy Spirit. The Christ who had spoken to them through His own lips now spoke to His people through the inspired speech of His servants! They called this continuing voice of Jesus in the church *prophecy*."[5]

How does God speak to a person? What do you do with those thoughts that God does share with you?

Prophecy in the early churches was expressed in various ways. During the services, any person on occasion could be inspired to speak forth the words of God (1 Cor. 14:1, 5, 31, 39). Also, some people were blessed with a charismatic gift of prophecy, so they could prophesy more readily and frequently (1 Cor. 12:10).

Finally, some in the church were called prophets, people particularly called to an advanced level of prophetic activity (Eph. 4:11). Outside the congregational meetings, the Christians were led of the Spirit, empowered to pray in the Spirit, and witnessed with the Spirit's power—indeed a prophetic people!

The non-Christian of Bible days came to the church gatherings because of the startling witness of some believing friend. The inquirer was spellbound by this God who was so wonderfully present and did such awesome things. The church felt God, experienced Him, yes, and heard His thoughts dynamically presented in a way that inspired them to live! May such things be restored to the churches today!

PERSONAL EXPERIENCE AND RELATIONAL SHARING

Let us explore three prophetic areas that are of particular interest. Each involves perceiving God's words and then using them wisely: personal experience, relational sharing, and congregational expression. The first two areas, personal and relational experience, do not always include speaking. They do involve hearing God's thoughts and wisely handling them, and this is foundational for every level of prophecy.

Prayer. It is of primary importance that prophetic people be prayerful, and this means both talking to God and hearing from God. A person who starts each day with worship and prayer becomes a candidate to share the thoughts of heaven. God delights in communicating His thoughts in an atmosphere of prayer and praise. (See Psalm 22:3; Revelation 19:10.) As Jack Hayford describes in *The Beauty of Spiritual Language*, dynamic prayer includes audible worship, Bible declarations, and fluent prayer in spiritual language (or tongues). (See 1 Corinthians 14:2.)[6]

God's voice. Some people are surprised that God will speak to them individually or speak in a church service, but this is what the Bible teaches. (See 1 Thessalonians 5:19–20; 1 Timothy 1:18; Revelation 2:7.)

From time to time, the Lord will bring personal insights about your family, job, personal life, or the situation of a friend. You will experience strong, clear, impressive words in your mind, which you realize are from God—and not your own thoughts. It will be like a sheep hearing the shepherd's voice. (See John 10.) Clear quotable words happen to Christians of various denominations, but unfortunately some think of such things as out of the ordinary and hardly ever happening. The experience can be lost because of neglect or unbelief.

> Some people are surprised that God will speak to them individually or speak in a church service, but this is what the Bible teaches.

Prophecy occurs because of: (1) seeing visions; (2) hearing God's voice; (3) experiencing spontaneous expression; (4) perceiving spiritual insight; and (5) receiving strong mental impression. The revelation that comes or the words that are spoken while a person is "in the Spirit" come not from reflection, premeditation, or study but are initiated by God for the benefit of His people. This revelation, Jack Hayford says, "occurs when a Christian either hears, sees or senses a prompting from the Holy Spirit and speaks what he or she has received."[7] Such things were standard operating procedure for the early church Christians, but not necessarily every day.

The difference between personal thought and spiritual revelation is illustrated in Matthew 16:16. Peter one moment declared something revealed by God ("Thou art the Christ, the son of the living God") and then within minutes gave his own blundering opinion (and received Jesus' rebuke). We are warned against being too overconfident: "Do not lay hands on anyone hastily" (1 Tim. 5:22).

Follow through. If you feel that God has shown you something personal, something for another person, or a prophetic word in church, seek wisdom to handle it correctly (James 1:5–8). Then, when communicating with others, think of yourself as a simple servant, not a great prophet. Although you may feel strongly impressed to share directly with an individual, resist imposing a heavy statement like: "I have a word from God for you!" Try humbly suggesting that you feel a burden or a desire to pray for them along certain lines. They, then, can confirm if the thought is really from God.

The early Christians were responsive to God's directives: Philip was directed by an angel and the Holy Spirit to the Ethiopian eunuch (Acts 8:26, 29). Peter was directed to Cornelius (Acts 10:19; 11:12). The prophet Agabus foretold a famine (Acts 11:28). The Spirit sent forth Paul and Barnabas (Acts 13:2). Paul was forbidden to preach the word in Asia (Acts 16:6).

"Do I have a prophetic gift?" Every Christian is gifted, but some are gifted prophetically (1 Cor. 12:4–11; Rom. 12:6). Would you be inclined to say yes to the following statements? (A *yes* ten times would be a strong indication of a prophetic gifting.)

- I am a born-again Christian, baptized in water, and baptized with the Holy Spirit.

- I practice a daily communion with God.

- I have experienced God speaking to me.

- I have experienced spiritual empowerment to prophesy, or share a thought from God, with positive results.

- I wish to do the will of God and wish to help others do the same.

- I wish to be wise in sharing God's thoughts.

- I would exercise faith to carry through in delivering God's message.

- I am cooperative with my pastoral leaders and sensitive to their advice about prophetic activity.

- I would evaluate with my pastor my track record with prophecy.

- Other Christians confirm this gifting in my life.

CONGREGATIONAL EXPRESSION

This third expression involves the church service setting and particularly fulfills the opening definition of prophecy.

The only record of the early charismatic meetings is given in 1 Corinthians 14, which deals with decorum in congregational gatherings. Paul's concern is that spiritual manifestations (particularly tongues, interpretation, and prophecy) are orderly and take place in an understandable, edifying manner.

Paul, a man who spoke in tongues more than anyone else (1 Cor. 14:18), was endued with very wise pastoral ability and prophetic insight. His best explanation of the practical purpose and function of prophecy is found in 1 Corinthians 14:3: "One who prophesies speaks to men for edification and exhortation and consolation" (NAS). Or, "One who prophesies is helping others grow in the Lord, encouraging and comforting them" (NLT).

Some churches are not structured to accommodate charismatic manifestations. The spontaneity of prophecy can be very unsettling to those accustomed to rigid program and procedure, and this is certainly understandable. But even churches that believe in prophecy must operate with reasonable structure and decorum, or the important balance between form and freedom will be lost. Churches that wisely allow for prophecy find such ministry most beneficial.

DECORUM IN SERVICES

There are various ways during congregational gatherings that prophecy can function beneficially, especially if the church has times of congregational prayer and Spirit-filled, Davidic-type worship. The most consistently workable and helpful approach is to train the people to wait until after the height of worship has been reached, then allow those who have prophetic ministry to come forward and speak their word clearly. In a large auditorium the use of a microphone is most appropriate. The simple screening of those who come forward to the microphone (or the policy of seeking permission from an elder) helps maintain a smooth service flow and eliminates any potential problems.

Many prophetic churches have ministry times of praying with or for the people. People on ministry teams find that prophetic insight often takes place. That insight is extremely helpful, but it need not always be given as a booming prophecy. A better use might be as a diplomatic, counseling tool in helping the person's faith find fulfillment.

Those who wish to be used in church services should be members of the church—godly, dedicated servants of God who truly wish to build up the local church. These people should discuss their gifting with the local leadership and prayerfully open themselves to advice on how to be used of God. Prayerful, dedicated living coupled with expectant faith is the best preparation for prophetic ministry.

PROPHETIC ACCURACY

Prophetic gifts and manifestations are protected and encouraged by evaluation and supervision. A congregation is at ease when they know that the church leadership will handle anything improper—and that the members will cooperate. Five biblical thoughts dictate the need for caution and supervision; they keep us aware that prophecy is not inerrant like Scripture, but it is extremely beneficial when safeguarded against error.

1. *To be judged (1 Cor. 14:29; 1 Thess. 5:20–21; 1 John 4:1)*—Like the traveling caravan salesman of biblical times who carried a small scale to weigh coins to check their authenticity, the church must also "judge" the prophecies given.

2. *Is in part [i.e., incomplete, only partial] (1 Cor. 13:9)*—This indicates that Corinthian or modern prophecy—unlike Scripture—was subject to possible error because the whole picture was not in view.

3. *Be encouraged (1 Cor. 14:1, 31, 39; Acts 2:17–18)*—Paul would not have encouraged everyone's participation in prophecy if he thought they would all be writing Scripture. Only a few apostle-prophets were inspired on a canonical prophecy level to write the New Testament Scriptures, and those writings alone would be accepted on a par with the Hebrew Scriptures as binding and authoritative. (See 1 Thessalonians 2:13; 2 Peter 3:16.) In contrast, as Cecil Robeck Jr. writes: "The

gift of prophecy seems to be designed by God to speak ad hoc, to specific people at specific times in specific situations."[8]

4. *Exercise faith (Rom. 12:6)*—The prophetic person must remember that prophecy operates "in proportion to our faith."

5. *Consider conditional (as in 1 Tim. 1:18)*—"If" clauses condition both prayer and prophecies. A study of Old Testament prophets shows that prophecy can be annulled, delayed, or suspended.

How wonderful it is to receive personal communication from God. His thoughts will inspire you, bless others, and build the churches. Small wonder that Paul said, "Do not despise prophecies" (1 Thess. 5:20), and "Therefore, brethren, desire earnestly to prophesy. . . . Let all things be done decently and in order" (1 Cor. 14:39–40).

About the Author

Ernest Gentile is the founding pastor of Christian Community Church in San Jose, California, which he began in 1959 and pastored for thirty-three years. Ernest has been active in conventions, minister's conferences, and prophetic conferences in the USA and abroad. Among other books, he is the author of *Your Sons & Daughters Shall Prophesy: Prophetic Gifts in Ministry Today* and *The Glorious Disturbance: Understanding and Receiving the Baptism With the Spirit*.

For Further Study

J. Rodman Williams, *The Era of the Spirit*

Ernest Gentile, *Your Sons & Daughters Shall Prophesy: Prophetic Gifts in Ministry Today*

Ernest Gentile, *Prophetic Presbytery in the Local Church*

CHAPTER 11

Despise Not Prophecy

—JACK W. HAYFORD

SUMMARY

Church leaders are called to encourage—and shepherd—the bittersweet gift of prophecy.

THE FIRE OF the Spirit awaits a place to break through in many of our churches today, and the spirit of prophecy—which always ultimately glorifies Jesus—must be allowed a place. There is nothing more desirable to the pursuit of a life lived in the fullness of the Spirit than prophecy—and neither is there anything less reliable. This paradox presses a dual responsibility upon each of us who lead among the Savior's flock. It reflects both a New Testament value that is too often denigrated and a realistic warning that is too seldom applied.

At Pentecost, through Simon Peter, the Holy Spirit breathed a timeless contemporizing of Joel's prophecy from the ninth century B.C.:

> "And it shall come to pass in the last days, says God, that I will pour out of My Spirit on all flesh; your sons and your daughters shall prophesy, your young men shall see visions, your old men shall dream dreams. And on My menservants and on My maidservants I will pour out of My Spirit in those days; and they shall prophesy." . . . For the promise is to you and to your children, and to all who are afar off, as many as the Lord our God will call.
>
> —ACTS 2:17–18, 39

In short, to put it in the nakedest of terms: this prophesying "thing" is not only here for today and here to stay. It is also being spread around by the free gifting of the Holy Spirit to be likely to happen to anyone in whom He dwells! It comes as a disappointment to many that likely human avenues for "prophesying" have such a limited criteria for their doing so.

To begin, there are no *maturity* qualifications. A prophet, as a servant of Christ fulfilling an office role under the Savior's appointment, does have to answer to the usual requirements incumbent on a spiritual leader such as blamelessness, temperance, sober-mindedness, hospitality, ability to teach, and so on (1 Tim. 3). However, it must be noted that to simply "prophesy" one does not have to meet such requirements.

Paul, assuming that many in the body would be used by the Spirit to share prophetic utterances from time to time, issues clear and expected directives that are to be followed when prophecies are given among saints in assembly:

> Let two or three prophets speak, and let the others judge. But if anything is revealed to another who sits by, let the first keep silent. For you can all prophesy one by one, that all may learn and all may be encouraged. And the spirits of the prophets are subject to the prophets. For God is not the author of confusion but of peace, as in all the churches of the saints.
> —1 CORINTHIANS 14:29–33

However, there aren't any restrictions on when, where, or how prophecies may be delivered. I'm certainly not saying I like this arrangement. I'm simply saying that God has been willing to open the door quite wide. I'm sure that's no argument for recklessness in the use of the gift of prophecy, and it in no way suggests a casual attitude toward its potential for confusing or misleading people.

But it seems certain that God must have a reason for this generous availability and liberality concerning its exercise. I believe it's because the vital, orderly function of the gift of prophecy is so much to be desired in the life of the local church. I hold to the principle that nothing more secures the life of the believer and the health of the local assembly than the solid, faithful, thoroughgoing teaching of the Word of God—the Holy Bible. This is His final written revelation—the authority by which all things are gauged and judged, by which the soul is saved, fed, and grown in health and strength unto glory.

So why "mess up" all this neatness with the possibility of distracting people from the Word of the Lord by uttering what they feel may be "a word from the

Lord"? Or worse, why does God offer an operative grace of the Spirit that can too easily be flavored or tainted by the flesh—or even a devil?

One reason this happens is because in its pure operation, the manifestation of the Holy Spirit in prophecies, as I have observed them through the years, demonstrates and tends to sustain a simplicity. I have often marveled at insights that come via the simplest vessels in our congregation—bursting brightness on the eternal Word as prophetic photographs of God's way are depicted in unstudied, simply quickened utterances that stir, awaken, and ignite hearts.

Faith, praise, humility, confession of sin, rejoicing, worship, comfort, and an awe of God are among a few of the responses I have seen produced by "a word" of prophecy. It may have taken no more than ninety seconds, but the sword-edge power of the Spirit's cutting through a moment with vibrating truth has often done more to advance the kingdom of God than the preceding three weeks of sermons.

Mind you, I'm not negating the value of steadfast teaching. I'm simply affirming facts an honest leader knows—and is willing to acknowledge. Because the truth is that—especially in the Western world—we are horribly prone to become enamored with our reasoned, intellectualized processing of God's Word through our systematic approaches to devotions, Bible teaching, preaching, and writing.

> I have often marveled at insights that come via the simplest vessels in our congregation—bursting brightness on the eternal Word as prophetic photographs of God's way are depicted in unstudied, simply quickened utterances that stir, awaken, and ignite hearts.

I am not trivializing the values of such, but my observation of the Holy Spirit's distributions of His gift of a prophetic word is that it's one way He uses to keep us humble. He often hereby reminds us that He can flow more through a baby than we can whomp up in a week; that He is still the Revealer, and He chooses to remind us that we aren't ultimately "in control" or "all that cool."

That's the part most of us don't like. (Let me whisper it so He can't hear: "I don't either.") Prophecies might be delivered in such sloppy or interruptive ways and, truth be told, are not always all that revealing and dynamic all that often! There are many that wander with words, others that seem redundant and unnecessary (and if they seem that way, they usually are).

But God still holds our feet to the fire with His own Word: "Do not quench the Spirit. Do not despise prophecies. Test all things; hold fast what is good" (1 Thess. 5:19–21). The verb *exoutheno* (despise) means "to make light of, to set at naught, to treat or reject with scorn." The text is a Holy Spirit commandment: don't mock, deride, or cheapen the place of prophecies in the body life of the church.

Such *despising*, however, is not only exercised when prophesying is disallowed, as some suppose. The definition above calls to responsibility as well as liberty. "Cheapening" is as unworthy as "despising," and it is an unquestionable fact that in many quarters today the ready flow of words that seems to excite a speaker or generate excitement might falsely be called "a prophetic word."

> But the fire of the Spirit awaits a place to break through in many of our churches today, and the spirit of prophecy—which always ultimately glorifies Jesus—must be allowed a place.

I've seen—we all have—meetings where temperatures run high, excitement rises to the rafters, exuberance becomes defined as anointing, and mere words are assumed to be the Spirit's word. The Bible—if we bother to get real with the whole of it—is pretty quick to close the gate on this kind of presumption as quickly as it mandates we keep the door open to prophecies.

The Holy Spirit's desire to fulfill three things—to edify (build up), exhort (stir up), and comfort (lift up)—is at the root of His insistence that we permit His availability to move even the simplest of Jesus' people in the simplest of ways and with the simplest of terms:

> But he who prophesies speaks edification and exhortation and comfort to men. He who speaks in a tongue edifies himself, but he who prophesies edifies the church.
>
> —1 CORINTHIANS 14:3–4

And where biblically focused and centered leaders lead spiritually humble and hungry saints in worship and into God's Word, there will and should always be an openness to "a word from the Lord."

It isn't my purpose in these few words to discuss the demanding and clearly specified requirements the New Testament gives concerning the character of those who give prophetic words. Nor is it my intention to fail the whole truth by not elaborating all that might be said about decency and order, and about judging prophecies, and about conformity to the plumb line of the Scriptures. All these things and more need to be heeded—heeded with a holy fear and righteous rigor.

But the fire of the Spirit awaits a place to break through in many of our churches today, and the spirit of prophecy—which always ultimately glorifies Jesus—must be allowed a place. Without His breaking through and breaking up, we're too vulnerable to finally breaking down. Or failing to be broken at all.

ABOUT THE AUTHOR

Jack W. Hayford, LittD, is the founding pastor of The Church On The Way in Van Nuys, California, chancellor of the King's College and Seminary, and president of the International Church of the Foursquare Gospel.

CHAPTER 12

Mission: Possible

—MATTHEW GREEN

SUMMARY

With the world at our doorstep and an almost unlimited supply of resources, the only ingredient missing in fulfilling the Great Commission is willing people.

THE CHURCH'S CENTER of gravity is changing. According to *The Expansion of Christianity* by missiologist Timothy Yates, in 1900, most Christians were in the "sending countries" of Europe and North America.[1] One hundred years later, in a proportion as high as sixty to forty, the balance has shifted to sub-Saharan Africa, Latin America, and the Pacific—Christendom's new center of gravity.

Yates also points out in his book that more than half of the world's two billion Christians are found in what were traditionally regarded as "mission fields." And the inhabitants of these mission fields are now being sent out as missionaries themselves.

The signs of growth worldwide indicate that today's Spirit-filled believers, in particular, are reaping the fruit of the evangelistic fervor of their forebears. Consider some statistics from Patrick Johnstone and Jason Mandryk's *Operation World*:

- In Latin America, the Pentecostal/Charismatic movement is challenging the hegemony of the Catholic Church and now accounts for 28 percent of the world's Pentecostals.

- In sub-Saharan Africa's growing African Independent Church (AIC) movement, Spirit-filled expressions of indigenous Christianity are the norm, making Christianity the dominant religion of that region.

- From China's burgeoning unregistered churches to the exploding congregations of South Korea, many of Asia's 130 million evangelicals would identify themselves as Pentecostal or Charismatic.[2]

NEW CHALLENGES

The expansion of the Pentecostal/Charismatic church worldwide may be attributed in part to the social context in which it has often sprouted. As Samuel Escobar explains in his book *The New Global Mission*, Pentecostalism has grown most rapidly among the socially marginalized and economically impoverished—sectors often overlooked in the church.

But he further notes, "After more than a century of existence and a process of institutionalization, several old Pentecostal churches are now middle or upper class in composition, thanks to the social mobility made possible by conversion experiences."[3]

Grant McClung agreed, suggesting that the movement has become "more sophisticated." "This may become a problem unless we catch more of the early spirit of the 'missionaries with a one-way ticket,'" he says, referring to the age when missionaries left for the field with no plans—or resources—to return home.[4]

McClung, the author of *Globalbeliever.com* and *Azusa Street and Beyond*, is field director for the Church of God Europe, overseeing the areas of Western Europe, the Mediterranean, and the Middle East. He is also associate professor of missions and church growth at the Church of God Theological Seminary in Cleveland, Tennessee.

While the missionaries of the nineteenth and early twentieth centuries confronted disease, primitive conditions, and geographical inaccessibility, the challenges of today are often more intangible.

David Shibley, founder and president of Global Advance, contends that militant Islam, postmodernism, and universalism pose as the three major worldviews at odds with the gospel. "While Communism is not the threat it once was, the philosophy behind it is still alive and kicking." He adds, "This is the challenge of materialism—a worldview that places great value on material things and little value on spiritual things."[5]

However, even in light of challenges such as these, one fact must be noted: the healthiest and most vibrant sectors of Christendom are those suffering the greatest economic, political, and social upheaval.

As Howard Foltz, professor of global evangelization at Regent University School of Divinity, notes, the growth of the church in countries such as China (the largest Communist nation in the world) and Indonesia (the largest Islamic nation in the world) is staggering. "Wherever there is persecution and hostility toward the gospel, the church is growing faster because of it," he contends.[6]

NEW MODELS

Missiologists argue that this unprecedented growth must be faced with a willingness on the part of the Western church to adjust traditional models of missions.

"Missions is no longer seen as solely the task of the Western church," Shibley says, noting that, as of the 1990s, more missionaries were deployed from non-Western nations than from Western nations. "It is the privilege of the worldwide church."[7]

The implication of these statistics is that, although the need still exists for pioneer missionaries and church planters, tomorrow's missionaries will be *partners* rather than *parents*. Foltz notes that the controller/director model, which dominated missions from the Colonial era to the late twentieth century, is being replaced by a servant/trainer model.

It is widely accepted that indigenous evangelists are more effective at reaching a culture than are outsiders. However, Western missions agencies have often been reluctant to release the reins and allow the national church to be self-supporting, self-propagating, and self-theologizing.

While there is always the real possibility that an indigenous church will end up looking a lot different than the typical Western counterpart, the importance of a culturally authentic expression of the gospel cannot be understated.

> But lest we labor under the assumption that money is the fuel of missions, the facts suggest that a commitment to spread the gospel often overcomes a seeming lack of resources.

"Too often, because American churches have had the financial resources, we have been too controlling overseas," McClung explains. "We need to set up new patterns of partnership with non-Western evangelists and missionaries in a final team effort to penetrate the darkness and finish the commission we were given."[8]

TECHNOLOGY

From the advent of the modern printing press—which many attribute to spawning the Protestant Reformation—to today's World Wide Web and satellite broadcasts, advancing technology has introduced new methods for completing the Great Commission.

For instance, David Shibley points out that perhaps the greatest twentieth-century evangelistic tool arrived in the form of the *JESUS* film, which has resulted in more than 176 million conversions.[9]

But technology's benefits can be deceptive at best and dangerous at worst. As Howard Foltz contends, "It is irrelevant to put typical Western teaching on the Web and send it around the globe thinking that it will relate to people in the 162 countries of the world—let alone the 12,000 people groups."[10]

Television, radio, books, and the Internet may end up doing more harm than good if they merely export a Western version of Christianity without allowing theology to sprout and be cultivated in an indigenous context.

David Shibley notes that—whether using the printing press or the satellite—Christians from Martin Luther to Billy Graham have harnessed technology to spread the gospel.[11]

However, citing the increasing global presence of Internet cafes and the educational opportunities that computers afford, he suggests that technology may more effectively be harnessed to serve the goals of training and discipleship.

But Shibley ultimately questions the suggestion that high-tech gadgetry will ever replace human contact. "The gospel will always remain relational at its roots," he says. "It takes breathing humans interacting with other breathing humans to experience the power of the resurrected Christ."[12]

Additionally, Foltz notes that the notion that radio, television, or Web broadcasts alone will reach unevangelized sectors of the globe is faulty.

"Just having the potential audience does not mean that they're listening," he contends. "And just because they're listening doesn't mean they understand."[13]

THE AMERICAN SCENE

The growth of the church overseas often begs the question, "What will become of the United States?" The overall cultural decline and lack of growth in many churches juxtaposed with a burgeoning demand for Christian books, music, television, and movies present a conundrum for the American evangelist.

Scott Hinkle, an evangelist based in Phoenix, suggests that the booming Christian subculture is no indication of substantive revival. "It merely reflects the trends of our culture and society," says the president of Soulwinners International, a ministry that trains people for evangelism. "We are inundated by information on every level, but it doesn't mean that we're being transformed at our roots—at our hearts."[14]

Some believe that the evangelistic fervor of the Pentecostal/Charismatic movement has waned. "Many people finance missions overseas," says James Davis, an Assemblies of God evangelist and president of the Global Pastors Network. "But merely giving is not the end result of what God has called us to be and to do. We are not gaining lost ground."[15]

> The signs of growth worldwide indicate that today's Spirit-filled believers, in particular, are reaping the fruit of the evangelistic fervor of their forebears.

And some question whether the church is really even digging deep to finance reaching the lost—let alone participating. "Only 2 percent of most churches' revenue goes to evangelism," Hinkle says. "We've become a 'remote control' society. If I pray and send a check, I've done the job."[16]

However, evangelists such as Davis and Hinkle are optimistic when they observe new trends toward cooperation among American churches. "Fences are falling, territorialism is dying, partnership is flourishing," Davis says. "But this will pose a greater challenge for the evangelist to find a place, a function."[17]

Although they admit that the public perception of the evangelist has taken a beating in recent years, both Hinkle and Davis point out that the stereotype of flamboyance and shady morals applied to evangelists can just as often be assigned to pastors.

"Because some evangelists are more in the media, we tend to remember their failures more than those of local pastors," Davis says. "But the impact of a pastor falling is greater than that of an evangelist—it's closer to home."[18]

Hinkle agrees and traces the stereotype to a lack of accountability that has sometimes characterized evangelists' ministries. "I've made it my practice to be a part of a local church," says Hinkle, who bases his ministry at Phoenix First Assembly and holds credentials with Christ for the Nations Institute.[19]

Davis encourages evangelists to pursue relationships that will offer accountability. "There needs to be guidelines and standards," he says. "And evangelists should stay away from the latest gimmicks and tricks of the trade."[20]

THE UNFINISHED TASK

A 2002 study conducted by the U.S. Center for World Mission (USCWM) acknowledged the global growth of the Christian faith, but confirmed two key concerns:[21]

The first is the growth of Islam as compared to that of the church. While strongly committed Christian groups (referred to in the study as "Great Commission Christians") are growing at a rate of 1.44 percent worldwide, Islam is expanding at 2.11 percent.

The second is the imbalance of resources devoted to evangelizing nominal Christians versus unreached people groups. Seventy-four percent of Protestant-missionary funds are supporting workers laboring among nominal Christian groups, versus 11 percent among Muslims, Buddhists, and Hindus, 8 percent among tribal people, 4 percent among the nonreligious, 2 percent among Chinese folk religions, and 1 percent among Jews.

As Howard Foltz notes, there is enough money to support the church, feed the hungry, and expand the kingdom exponentially...if the majority of Christians would merely tithe. Foltz cites George Barna's notoriously depressing 2000 stewardship study that indicated only 9 percent of evangelicals tithe.[22]

It could be argued that Christians feel a lack of confidence when giving—wondering how much of their hard-earned money is actually going to evangelizing the unreached and how much is being spent on propping up institutional structures in the Western world.

For instance, the USCWM study notes that the church spends more money dealing with "ecclesiastical crime" than is spent on foreign missions—$18 billion, versus $17 billion. And the $17 billion spent on missions is only .001 percent of the Christian church's total annual income of $15.5 trillion.[23]

But lest we labor under the assumption that money is the fuel of missions, the facts suggest that a commitment to spread the gospel often overcomes a seeming lack of resources. Take, for instance, two nations that have come to the forefront in sending missionaries worldwide: Nigeria and South Korea.

With an average annual income of $280 per person (.9 percent of the income per person in the United States), most Nigerian believers are challenged to keep food on the table, yet, in Operation World, Patrick Johnstone estimates that 3,700 Nigerian missionaries are working in more than 50 countries.[24]

Or consider that South Korean believers, with an average income of $10,550 per person (34 percent of the income per person in the United States), are currently supporting more than 12,000 missionaries in 156 countries.[25]

USCWM further confirms that if money were the key to converting unbelievers, the United States would be a veritable hotbed of revival. While an average of $1,400 is spent to reach every new convert in Mozambique, it takes $1.5 million to convert and baptize one American.[26]

The passion and initiative for global evangelism embraced by the global church are indications that the unfinished task of the Great Commission will be accomplished. But Western believers must adopt a spirit of flexibility and humility, building long-term partnerships and practicing servanthood.

As Foltz notes, the goal of a missionary should always be analogous to that of a farmer. "Dig deep, plough a straight furrow, go far," he says. "Don't think merely about sowing the seed—think about the harvest."[27]

ABOUT THE AUTHOR

Matthew D. Green served for four years as editor of *Ministry Today* magazine. He is currently a freelance writer and director of communications for Pioneers, a mission agency supporting more than one hundred eighty church-planting teams among unreached people groups in eighty-two countries. His Web site may be found at www.matthewdgreen.com.

FOR FURTHER STUDY

David Shibley, *The Missions Addiction*

Howard Foltz, *For Such a Time As This: Strategic Missions Power Shifts for the 21st Century*

L. Grant McClung, *Globalbeliever.com: Connecting to God's Work in Your World*

James O. Davis, *The Pastor's Best Friend: The New Testament Evangelist*

CHAPTER 13

Ministerial Etiquette

—BRENDA KUNNEMAN

SUMMARY

The evangelist's relationship with the local church doesn't have to be tense. Here's a biblical model for a healthy—and productive—partnership between itinerant ministers and the churches they serve.

WITH SO MANY churches and ministries springing up almost overnight, it is no surprise that we have a number of differing ideas on what is considered ministerial etiquette between pastors and traveling ministers. Etiquette in ministry covers a broad spectrum of issues, but one area needing some clear guidelines is how pastors and traveling ministers should plan meetings and conferences.

Pastors and itinerate ministers often view several things differently. Yet they can avoid miscommunication by learning to understand each other and to work together. Most ministries, whether pastoral or evangelistic, want to represent themselves with excellence. Perhaps knowing some basic principles found in Romans 12 can help. Most of us are familiar with these truths, but in the daily work of ministry they can get overlooked.

1. Show genuine love (Rom. 12:9).

2. Show honor by putting the other ministry's needs first (Rom. 12:10).

3. Show organization and diligence in ministry business (Rom. 12:11).

4. Give freely to another whatever is needed (Rom. 12:13).

5. Show welcoming hospitality (Rom. 12:13).

6. Be considerate to ease the load of one another's burdens (Rom. 12:15).

7. Have regard for others and be harmonious (Rom. 12:16).

8. Be content, and don't think of your ministry as more important than another's (Rom. 12:16).

9. Show honesty and integrity in all dealings (Rom. 12:17).

10. Take responsibility to keep peace (Rom. 12:18).

11. Drop any grievance or offense (Rom. 12:19).

12. Do good at all times (Rom. 12:21).

Let's apply these principles to some everyday situations that will help pastors and itinerate evangelists know what is considered proper etiquette for working together.

SHOWING GENUINE LOVE

Showing love begins with knowing the true reason why we hold conferences and host guest speakers. The answer is, of course, to meet the needs of people. It is not to promote names, make money, or gain exposure for ourselves or our ministry.

Even though there is a proper perspective concerning success in ministry, the devil loves to pervert it, turning our focus away from Jesus and onto ourselves. Genuine love reminds us that our ministry is for the Lord and those who need Him. As ministers, this attitude must be real, not fabricated. Anyone can put on a front, but we need to search our hearts to know whether our love is genuine or our motives have been clouded by personal achievement. Wrong motives will eventually cause us to become selfish as we arrange events.

PUTTING OTHERS' MINISTRY FIRST

Itinerate ministries, and even churches, should have a list of travel directives they give one another when planning meetings. It should include information regarding necessary travel arrangements, instructions for product sales, and other accommodations.

This reduces confusion for both the host and guest and keeps things functioning smoothly. Depending on the size of the ministry, these provisions can vary extensively. Some larger itinerate ministries unavoidably require more when they come. Therefore, not every traveling ministry/church relationship is a good match. Some churches are not able (either financially or in manpower) to handle an overextended list of demands.

If the Lord has called you to work with a church for an event, always think of the other ministry's unique needs and be considerate. Keep expectations reasonable for your ministry's size. While a church may be able to cover expenses for the itinerate minister and one assistant, it is probably not right to ask for much more. That does not mean you have to constantly do without important things; just be polite.

> Many churches don't make sacrificial steps of faith to be generous with guest speakers. Perhaps they don't consider the demands and numerous challenges of constant travel and life in a hotel.

Some itinerates fail to think of the financial strain many pastors face to host them, or how much work is required of the church staff to hold the meeting. Pastors of smaller churches may only be able to afford a minimal list of ministries during a year, while a sizeable, well-established church might be able to handle more. Therefore, keep your needs realistic and workable for all the different types of ministries you may deal with.

In turn, many churches don't make sacrificial steps of faith to be generous with guest speakers. Perhaps they don't consider the demands and numerous challenges of constant travel and life in a hotel. In addition, a guest may not always know what to expect upon arrival at a new church. That guest's role is very different from that of the pastor, who knows what to expect each week in his own church.

In everything you plan, do what benefits everyone. Pastors should be willing to do all they can to meet a guest's needs, and, in turn, itinerates should be polite with their requests. Avoid thinking that the needs and success of your ministry are more important than someone else.

HOSPITALITY AND GENEROSITY

The foundation of good itinerate/pastor relationships lies in a generous attitude. Most ministries agree that churches should cover the basic list of expenses, which includes airfare/mileage, hotel, and meals for the meetings. So what remains is determining how extravagant or practical these expenses should be and what extras should be considered. All ministries need to be both generous and reasonable at the same time. Remember that money spent in ministry is for the kingdom of Christ, sowed by God's people, and should be used wisely.

For example, we had a guest in our church who spoke on a Sunday at both morning and evening services. He planned to leave immediately after the evening service. After the morning meeting we told him we would take him to his hotel, but he insisted on spending the afternoon preparing for service at the church office so there wouldn't be another hotel expense for a room only being used during the day. We would have never expected that, and we tried to convince him otherwise, but he was determined about it in an effort to be a good steward of God's resources.

Since itinerates spend so much time in hotels, their hosts should do all they can to make each hotel stay a pleasure instead of a challenge. Choose hotel accommodations that are comfortable and well above the economy hotel standard (unless nothing else is available in your town). This does not mean you must spend absolute top dollar, but you should stretch beyond average. Leave a gift or food basket, and be sensitive to their preferences.

Many freedoms and conveniences one is used to at home are not available when traveling. Be thoughtful about what they like to eat and when they prefer their meals. For example, a guest speaker may not want to eat with your church members at the all-church dinner after a service. Also give thought to the vehicle used to pick them up at the airport. Is it clean, large enough, warm, or cool?

At the service, have ushers available to help them before and after the meeting. Unless requested otherwise, don't leave them alone to mingle among the congregation before and after the services, where they could be subjected to a host of things. Not every person who might approach them knows how to be respectful.

INTEGRITY IN OFFERINGS AND HONORARIUMS

We probably don't want to think of ministry in monetary terms, but it takes money to do anything. Most itinerate ministries come to churches without requiring a set *fee* or honorarium. Instead, they come for a freewill offering to be received at each service, which is probably the best etiquette for most occasions.

Many smaller traveling ministries depend upon offerings just to pay bills. For example, a smaller traveling ministry may average two to four meetings a month, and in many cases less. Many reputable pastors agree that traveling ministers should typically receive an average offering of $1000 per service. This number is an average and will vary for smaller or larger congregations, but it is a good number to begin with.

Based on that figure, if the traveling minister stayed at each church for two days of meetings, and did about thirty-five meetings per year, it adds up to about $70,000 per year. That amount needs to cover salary(s) and overhead for the ministry such as nonreimbursed travel, work overseas, production, postage, printing, and office expenses.

That estimate only works if the itinerates actually receive that much in each service and have that many meetings a year. Many traveling ministers receive less and end up wondering how they will pay their bills. This is particularly discouraging, especially when they put their hearts into the meetings.

We have encouraged our congregation to ask themselves this question: "If every household gave what you give, would our guest speaker be blessed?" For example, in the average American church of fifty families (a good average for many), if each family gave $25 to the guest, the speaker would receive a total of $1250 from that church. They would likely need to duplicate that amount four times that month to keep the overhead covered.

When you add travel days, this also means they will be gone half the month and then still need to find time for family and office work. Some have partner support, but that may not be sufficient in every case. Thinking in these practical terms helps churches and pastors know the importance of blessing the guest ministries they invite.

These figures do not apply generally to much larger ministries or churches, and there are exceptions to everything. However, the larger the ministry becomes, the greater the demands, national expectations, expenses, and even criticism. Some national ministries are keeping up with the load of fulfilling hundreds of preaching invitations each year. So regardless of ministry size, pastors must teach their congregations how to properly give to guest speakers.

In addition, when a pastor receives an offering specifically for a guest speaker, then 100 percent of that offering should undoubtedly go to the speaker. It should never be divided to cover expenses for the meeting. Sadly, some churches have adopted this practice. The only exception might be if the guest requested to sow an offering for expenses back into the church. We have had pastors tell us after a service that since the offering was good, they were going to subtract travel expenses, even though that was not agreed upon.

> When a pastor receives an offering specifically for a guest speaker, then 100 percent of that offering should undoubtedly go to the speaker. It should never be divided to cover expenses for the meeting.

One time we ministered in a service with about two hundred people in attendance. We were given our *offering* in a paper bag containing cash and coin, which amounted to $400. A little surprised by the paper bag, we mentioned it to some of our staff members who happened to attend the meeting. We found that some of them had written checks, which together totaled nearly $400. So what happened to the rest? We can only guess. Pastors who split offerings when their people gave expecting the amount they gave to go to the guest are misleading their church.

BE ORGANIZED

Organization is an extremely important part of every ministry. We all make mistakes, but constant tardiness, unreturned phone calls, missed flights, and calendar mishaps, among other things, create difficulties with the other ministry you are working with.

Years ago, at a church where we were ministering, about forty-five minutes into the service the pastor had not yet arrived. I feel strongly about participating in the praise service, so we came in on time. He finally entered, almost an hour late. He hadn't seen us since we arrived, so it created a scene during worship while he greeted us on the front row.

Ministers should enter the sanctuary within the first few minutes of service to be an example in honoring our Lord, as well as honoring the musicians who are ministering. It also keeps the people from being distracted later in the service.

Last minute conference planning should not be normal practice. Sometimes we receive requests to hold last minute meetings at our church as people "get a word to come." These can be hard to administrate and budget for, and we usually prefer not to do them. That doesn't mean we cannot obey a sudden instruction from God to plan a conference, but we are aware that it is difficult to carry out effective ministry on a whim.

When planning the finances, product sales, arrivals and departures, advertising, and so on, do everything orderly and with time to spare. It is best to make travel directives and other pertinent information available approximately one month prior to the meeting.

There are times when mishaps occur, so be understanding. While it should be rare to cancel meetings, both pastors and traveling ministers need to afford each other occasional liberties to make calendar changes. All of us have planned some things that seemed good at the time but felt uneasy later. Perhaps it was just a timing or financial issue, but it happens. We are all doing our best to hear from the Lord. If you must make a calendar change, if at all possible, do it well in advance, so the other ministry does not incur unnecessary expenses. If expenses are incurred, offer to help cover them.

Pulpit Manners

Both pastors and itinerate ministers must stay sensitive to what is acceptable in the pulpit. A good pastor/guest speaker relationship will thrive when both parties handle the pulpit with integrity. First, pastors should prepare their people in advance to anticipate a move of God. Creating a receptive atmosphere before the guest arrives will make it easier for there to be a flow of the anointing. If you do not do this, your people will come inquisitive rather than ready to receive.

Guest speakers should remember that true shepherds are protective and love their flocks. Therefore, they should handle the church pulpit respectfully. There are some things that guests would be wise to avoid in a pastor's pulpit. This list may not include all such things, but it covers most:

- Always honor the pastor. Never directly correct him/her in front of his congregation. It is also good manners to thank the church publicly for having you.

- Be careful what you prophesy publicly to a pastor. Some personal information about him or his family should be kept private. This really

99

applies to everyone, but pastors, in particular, do not need church members constantly bringing up a prophecy that may have been personal in content. Avoid embarrassing people.

- Don't *test out* some new or unusual revelation from the pulpit. Doctrines should be submitted previously to your trusted ministerial relationships.

- Be cautious about acting out unusual demonstrations of the spirit. That doesn't mean you can't step out in faith; just be wise to prevent embarrassing yourself. For example, an individual may not appreciate having a whole bottle of oil dumped over his or her head. That results in nothing but a mess!

- Never receive offerings or partner sign-ups without the pastor's OK before the service. If he gives you the green light, then handle it with integrity.

- Don't make it your mission to overhaul the entire direction of a church. Preach the Word, which may cause them to stretch. Just don't make your vision their vision.

- Be adaptable to their style of ministry. Ministers differ on numerous ministry styles (songs, order of service, expression, and so on), and these differences have little to do with overall credibility. This applies to both pastors and itinerates.

MAKE PEACE AND DO GOOD

The most valuable key of all in ministry relationships is to stay in love with each other. When offenses arise, drop them, forgive, and move on. Truthfully, some ministries won't operate well together, but the important thing is to stay unified with the body of Christ and speak kindly of other ministries. Ultimately, let your life and ministry give glory to the Lord, and He will teach us all how to handle ourselves better as we grow in Christ.

ABOUT THE AUTHOR

Brenda Kunneman is cofounder and vice president of One Voice Ministries (www.onevm.org) and pastors Lord of Hosts World Outreach with her husband, Hank. Brenda travels periodically conducting conferences and crusades.

She also travels with her husband, and together they flow in tongues and interpretation as well as demonstrations of the Holy Spirit.

FOR FURTHER STUDY

James O. Davis, *The Pastor's Best Friend: The New Testament Evangelist*

CHAPTER 14

How to Share Your Faith (Without Losing Your Mind)

—RAY COMFORT

SUMMARY

Do you hate witnessing? If so, you're not alone, but the problem may not be with you—it may be that your message is not biblical.

ONE OF MY neighbor's kids fell into his swimming pool the other day. I was waxing my new car at the time, and as the two-year-old began to drown, I couldn't help but think how blessed I was to have such a nice vehicle. Just waxing it and giving it a shine made me burst with pride. I *love* my car, and I *love* the pleasure it gives me.

Of course, the above incident didn't happen. How could anyone let a child drown because he is preoccupied with waxing his car! Such a person would be guilty of the crime of "depraved indifference." It is against the law to fail to help another human being who is in mortal danger.

In his book *The Coming Revival*, Bill Bright said that only 2 percent of the church in America regularly share their faith with others.[1] That means that 98 percent of the professed body of Christ in America may be guilty of the sin of depraved indifference. They wax bold in worship and couldn't care less that the world is sinking into hell. Love could never ignore a drowning child, and love cannot preoccupy itself with the pleasures of worship and have no concern that every day 150,000 people are swallowed by death.

Charles Spurgeon said, "Do you have no wish for others to be saved? Then you are not saved yourself, be sure of that." Let's hope that you are not in that category. Rather, let's trust that you simply needed to be reminded of your moral responsibility to reach out to the lost and that from today on you are going to do something about it.

Still, you may have a very real fear of approaching strangers and talking about the things of God. There is also the thought that if you do approach someone, you don't want to blow it. These thoughts combine into one big, cold, unattractive, ever-increasing snowball. Strangers are hard enough to approach. What do you say to someone you don't know? But how about your neighbors? They are even harder to approach (if that's possible). If you make a mess of witnessing to your neighbors, you could start a lifetime feud. Then there's your mother-in-law. Upsetting her could cause really big problems.

> Love could never ignore a drowning child, and love cannot preoccupy itself with the pleasures of worship and have no concern that every day 150,000 people are swallowed by death.

These are fears that all of us have, and they are very real. However, there are certain principles that can help us to bring our fears into perspective. Think of what you fear. It is probably a fear of rejection—of feeling foolish.

Now think of the terrible fate of those who die in their sins. They will go to hell forever. It is no contest. We have no choice. When it comes to evangelism, we have a similar responsibility to that of a firefighter. Think of his moral obligation as he looks at the mother screaming for help from a six-story building. He mustn't listen to his fears, and you must deal with your fears in light of the sinner's horrifying fate.

Here are some simple suggestions for getting started. Practice being friendly. Talk with people. Try it at the park, at the gas station, or at the grocery store. Perhaps you already have an outgoing and friendly personality, but if you tend to be shy and introverted, try to open up a little and start talking with people. A simple, "Hi, how are you?" isn't hard. "Nice day isn't it? My name is so and so."

With a bit of practice, anyone can learn to be friendly. Most people respond warmly to warmth. Once we see that this is true, it will help to calm our fear-filled imaginations. Someone e-mailed our ministry and told us about how he and a friend went to the park on a Saturday afternoon just to practice being friendly to strangers. They had so much fun that they couldn't wait to get out the next weekend to take the next step.

After you have gained a measure of confidence in simply being friendly and talking to people, you are ready to learn the next step—how to swing the conversation to the subject of spiritual things. Charles Spurgeon also said, "If you would win souls, you must seek them. The sportsman knows that his game will not come to the window of his house to be shot. The fisherman knows that the fish will not come swimming up to his house." So don't wait for the fish to come to you. John 4 is our God-given example of personal witnessing. So let's look to the way of the Master to see how it's done.

If you take a moment to read the chapter, you will notice that Jesus spoke to the woman at the well when she was alone. We will often find that people are more open and honest when they are alone. So, if possible, pick a person who is sitting by himself.

From John 4 we can see four clear principles to follow.

1. Jesus began in the natural realm (v. 7).

The woman at the well of Samaria was unregenerate. The Bible tells us, "The natural man does not receive the things of the Spirit of God" (1 Cor. 2:14). Therefore, Jesus spoke to her of something to which she could relate—water. Most of us can strike up a conversation with a stranger in the natural realm. Besides, by now you have been practicing, and you know that you can do it. It may be a friendly, "How are you doing?" or a warm "Good morning!" If the person responds with a sense of warmth, ask, "Do you live around here?" From there develop a conversation.

2. Jesus swung the conversation to the spiritual realm (v. 10).

Jesus simply mentioned the things of God. This will take courage. We may say something like, "Did you go to church on Sunday?" or "Did you see that Christian TV program last week?" Perhaps you could ask the question I find to be very helpful. I say, "Did you see Mel Gibson's movie *The Passion of the Christ*?" Millions saw the movie, and even if they didn't see it, it opens the way for the next question: "Do you have a Christian background?" This will inoffensively probe his background. I have asked this thousands of times and have found that people are not at all offended.

Most people like talking about their favorite subject—themselves. He may answer, "I went to church when I was a child, but I drifted away from it." Another simple way to swing to the spiritual is to offer the person a gospel tract (we have plenty of interesting tracts available through our ministry) and ask, "Did you get one of these?" When he takes it, simply say, "It's a gospel tract. Do you come from a Christian background?"

3. Jesus brought conviction using the law of God (vv. 16–18).

Here is a vital part of witnessing that most people miss. It is a great mistake to sow seed onto hard soil. That will produce a disappointing crop. Instead, a wise farmer turns the soil before he plants his precious seed. He breaks up the soil so that it can accept the seed. The same applies spiritually. It is a great error to plant the precious seed of the gospel on the hard, unregenerate heart of humanity. That will produce a disappointing crop. Instead, we should do what Jesus did and use the Moral Law (the Ten Commandments) to prepare the way of the gospel.

> The way to find out a person's spiritual state is simply to ask the question, "Would you consider yourself to be a good person?" You will be surprised to find that people are not offended by this.

This is what Jesus did in Mark 10:17, Luke 18:18, and other places. The biblical rule of thumb is, "Law to the proud and grace to the humble." If someone has a humble heart and knows he has sinned against God, that person is ready for grace (such as the case of Nathaniel, Nicodemus, and Cornelius).

But if he is an average person—one who is proud and self-righteous—he will need the Law to humble him. This was the case with this sexually promiscuous woman in the fourth chapter of John. Jesus gently spoke directly to her conscience by alluding to the fact that she had transgressed the seventh commandment. He used the Law to bring "the knowledge of sin." (See Roman 3:19–20.)

The way to find out people's spiritual state is simply to ask the question, "Would you consider yourself to be a good person?" You will be surprised to find that people are not offended by this. If they say no (which is highly unlikely), ask them what they mean. Remember, you are asking them about their favorite subject—themselves.

Most likely you'll find that they are kidding, or that they've done something in their life that they feel bad about. Otherwise, expect them to say, "I'm a pretty good person," or "I'm a *really* good person." (See Proverbs 20:6 for the reason people respond in this way.) Such a response reveals a person's proud self-righteous attitude. Now you are ready to use the Law to humble that person—the same way Jesus did (Mark 10:17–22).

Next, ask, "Do you think that you have kept the Ten Commandments?" Most people think they have, so quickly follow with, "Have you ever told a lie?" This *is* confrontational, but if it's asked in a spirit of love and gentleness, there won't be any offense. Remember that the "work of the Law [is] written in their hearts" and that the conscience will bear "witness" (Rom. 2:15).

Jesus confronted the rich young ruler in Luke 18:18–21 with five of the Ten Commandments, and there was no offense. Have confidence that the conscience will do its work and affirm the truth of each commandment. Don't be afraid to gently ask, "Have you ever stolen something, even if it's small?" Learn how to open up the spirituality of the Law and show how God considers lust to be the same as adultery (Matt. 5:27–28) and hatred the same as murder (1 John 3:15).

Make sure you get an admission of guilt. Ask the person, "If God judges you by the Ten Commandments on Judgment Day, do you think you will be innocent or guilty?" If he says he will be innocent, ask, "Why is that?" If he admits his guilt, ask, "Do you think you will go to heaven or hell?" From there the conversation may go in one of the following three ways:

He may confidently say, "I don't believe in hell."

If so, gently respond, "That doesn't matter. You still have to face God on Judgment Day whether you believe in it or not. If I step onto the freeway when a massive truck is heading for me, and I say, 'I don't believe in trucks,' my lack of belief isn't going to change reality."

Then tenderly tell him he has *already* admitted to you that he has lied, stolen, and committed adultery in his heart. Let him know that God gave him a conscience so that he would know right from wrong. His conscience and the conviction of the Holy Spirit will do the rest. That's why it is essential to draw out an admission of guilt *before* you mention Judgment Day or the existence of hell.

He may say that he's guilty, but that he will go to heaven.

This is usually because he thinks that God is "good" and that He will, therefore, overlook sin in his case. Point out that if a judge in a criminal case has a guilty murderer standing before him, the judge, if he is a good man, can't just let him go. He must ensure that the guilty man is punished. If God is good, He must (by nature) punish murderers, rapists, thieves, liars, adulterers, fornicators, and those who have lived in rebellion to the inner light that God has given to every man.

He may admit that he is guilty and therefore going to hell.

Ask him if that concerns him. Speak to him about how much he values his eyes and how much more therefore he should value the salvation of his soul.

4. Jesus revealed Himself to her (v. 26).

Once the Law has humbled the person, he is ready for grace. Remember, the Bible says that God resists the proud and gives grace to the humble (James 4:6). The gospel is for the humble (Luke 4:18). Only the sick need a physician, and only those who will admit that they have the disease of sin will truly embrace the cure of the gospel. Learn how to present the work of the cross—that God sent His Son to suffer and die in our place.

Tell the sinner of the love of God in Christ, that Jesus rose from the dead and defeated death. Take him back to civil law and say, "It's as simple as this: we broke God's law, and Jesus paid our fine. If you will repent and trust in the Savior, God will forgive your sins and dismiss your case." Ask him if he understands what you have told him. If he is willing to confess and forsake his sins, and trust the Savior with his eternal salvation, have him pray and ask God to forgive him. Then pray for him. Get him a Bible. Instruct him to read it daily and to obey what he reads. Encourage him to get into a Bible-believing, Christ-preaching church.

ABOUT THE AUTHOR

Ray Comfort is the founder of Living Waters Ministries (www.livingwaters .org), which is dedicated to providing evangelistic resources for believers. He also coproduces (with Kirk Cameron) *The Way of the Master*, a television series offering practical insight for sharing one's faith. Ray is the author of numerous books, including *Hell's Best Kept Secret* and *What Hollywood Believes: An Intimate Look at the Faith of the Famous*.

FOR FURTHER STUDY

Ray Comfort (with Kirk Cameron), *The Way of the Master: How to Share Your Faith Simply, Effectively, Biblically—the Way Jesus Did*

Ray Comfort, *Hell's Best Kept Secret*

Ray Comfort, *What Did Jesus Do?*

CHAPTER 15

The World Is Waiting

—REINHARD BONNKE

SUMMARY

We are called to be "out and about," but the church has forgotten its reason for existence: the lost.

WOULDN'T IT BE wonderful if life were like a flight simulator: all of the excitement, none of the risk; all of the pleasure, none of the expense? But as author and philosopher Francis Bacon once wrote, "Simulation is a pretense of what is not." Sometimes it seems as though the church has taken a cue from modern technology, living in a simulated world where we go through the motions of faith with our chairs stuck firmly to the floor. While it would be easier to reach the world through some evangelistic equivalent of the flight simulator, the operative word in the Great Commission is *go*.

In places such as Africa, it is a no man's land of riots and civil wars. Converts face a menacing world much like the first Christians faced. If Christian joy comes from persecution, thousands in today's emerging countries know the original thing. But, are we here in the Western world actually going and experiencing, or are we merely going through the motions? When Jesus came, He went everywhere with His disciples. Some may think that through our prayers we can send the Lord to save the nations, but the reality is that we must go for Him. (See Isaiah 6:8.)

111

Until the Son of God came to earth, the only nation with knowledge of God—Israel—believed they had Jehovah enshrined behind the curtain of the holy of holies in the temple in Jerusalem. But when Jesus died, that curtain was ripped from top to bottom. This supernatural event served as public notice from God that He was "out and about," not confined to a temple. He belongs to the whole world.

FRUITLESS MOTION

Many prepare for evangelistic work by attending seminars and conferences, filling their notebooks, listening to sermons and Bible studies. They are dedicated to gathering knowledge. But as perpetual students, they may never leave class to practice what they've learned. For instance, a young man once told me that he belonged to a youth group that held "indoor open-air meetings," simulated street events, complete with heckling actors. Churches may make a show of interest, busy with activities, meetings, sessions, and business—keeping things going, but ultimately standing still.

> There is no substitute for the cross, whether miracles, phenomena, music, eloquence, or positive thinking. The most significant event in all history, Christ's crucifixion, is too shattering not to matter.

Israel's army under Saul made plenty of noise, brandished their weapons, and looked fierce, but only one teenage youngster named David ended up doing the fighting. One church I heard of called itself "a center of continuous evangelism" but saw only one convert per year. We may take up the pose, keep the church machine in vigorous motion, while the agenda of the board has no item relevant to Christ's agenda—the Great Commission. However, we must remember that the fire of evangelism cannot be ignited through artificial or humanly orchestrated means.

THE "CROSS FIRE"

In ancient Israel, the altar fire had been lit by an act of God. But two sons of Aaron offered "unholy fire" in their incense burners, and "fire came out from the presence of the LORD and devoured them" (Lev. 10:1–2, RSV). Artificial fire such as this does not please the heart of the Father.

God must kindle in us the eternal love that burned on the altar of Calvary. Today, the message of the cross is entrusted to the church. All the church's seats may be full, people attracted by multiple interests, social popularity, splendid services, or even selected Bible teaching—meanwhile, Jesus hangs on the cross without their particular attention.

Church zeal can be false fire. As Paul told the Corinthians, he preached with "love unfeigned"—passionate reality (2 Cor. 6:6, KJV). The cross is stamped across Scripture's pages, and preaching without the cross is not the gospel. Paul expressed his Christianity by saying, "For I determined not to know anything among you except Jesus Christ and Him crucified" (1 Cor. 2:2). There is no substitute for the cross, whether miracles, phenomena, music, eloquence, or positive thinking. The most significant event in all history, Christ's crucifixion, is too shattering not to matter.

While I suppose every church in the land holds the cross of Christ in special regard, what does it mean to them? A preacher once suggested that "Christ died because He believed in us—that we were worth dying for." This ideology reverses the truth of the cross! The cross is a spectacle that brings us to tears, shames us, and stands as an example of selflessness and integrity.

Isaac Watts, in his hymn "When I Survey the Wondrous Cross," writes:

> Love so amazing, so divine,
> Demands my soul, my life, my all.[1]

But is that why Jesus gave His life—just to shame us, challenge us, or bring grief to our eyes? No, this love was demonstrated to save us when we could not save ourselves.

WHY WE EXIST

Paul spoke of the "offense of the cross" (Gal. 5:11). The offense is the proclamation of Christ's blood spilled for our sins. This offense ceases when Jesus is preached as merely a victim or martyr. Instead, He embraced death, taking up our cause at such frightful cost. It is not that we are saved when we see the cross. Instead, we are saved when God the Father sees the cross—the transaction of redemption. Jesus said, "This is my blood...shed for many for the remission of sins" (Matt. 26:28).

When the cross is preached in terms that decorate it with sentiment, it is stripped of its saving power. Paul did not preach to the Romans about the

Jesus they had just executed merely to make them feel sorry about it. He preached it as the hope of their salvation. When Peter charged the Jews in Acts 2:23 that "you, with the help of wicked men, put him to death by nailing him to the cross" (NIV), he didn't reproach them, but declared that Jesus' death had intrinsic meaning—cleansing power for the forgiveness of sins.

Ultimately, the cross reminds us of why we exist as the church and the price that was paid for us and for those who have not yet heard. We are here on earth to spread the message of the cross, to move from the simulated reality that the Christian life can often become, to be "out and about" as Jesus was, burning with a consuming fire for the lost.

ABOUT THE AUTHOR

The founder of Christ for All Nations (www.cfan.org), Reinhard Bonnke was ordained by the German Pentecostal Church and has served as a pastor, a missionary, and an evangelist.

FOR FURTHER STUDY

Reinhard Bonnke, *Even Greater*

Reinhard Bonnke, *Evangelism by Fire: Igniting Your Passion for the Lost*

Reinhard Bonnke, *Mighty Manifestations: The Gifts and Power of the Holy Spirit*

CHAPTER 16

Man on Fire: A Q&A With Reinhard Bonnke
—MATTHEW GREEN

SUMMARY

Reinhard Bonnke has the fiery passion and fatherly compassion that make up the ingredients of a biblical evangelist.

WHEN HE IS trying to get a point across, Reinhard Bonnke is known for his colorful metaphors—comparing evangelism to arson (in a good way), the church to a pleasure boat (in a bad way), and his style of ministry to sugar mixed with sand. But the descriptive word that most who know him would use to describe Bonnke is *fiery*.

The same inner flame that burns as this stocky evangelist persuades crowds of more than a million in open-air crusades smolders as he shares his calling, seated at his desk at his Orlando, Florida–based ministry, Christ for All Nations (CfaN).

"I may come across as being a person of passion," he admits. "But my passion is tempered with divine compassion. This compassion is what makes an evangelist."

No, Bonnke is not an evangelist enamored with visions of hellfire and brimstone, whose very presence in the room makes people doubt their salvation. Rather, he possesses the single-minded, white-hot burden for the lost that tends to spread to whoever hears him speak—not by using guilt, but inspiring others with his longing to see souls brought into the kingdom.

Just since 2000, Bonnke has preached to fifty million people, and CfaN has documented thirty-four million decisions for Christ through follow-up cards. But after nearly forty-five years of ministry, the German-born evangelist has no plans to take a "holiday" any time soon.

While crusade attendees report healings—from the disappearance of tumors to the restoration of sight—some have experienced miracles without even attending Bonnke's crusades.

> Biblical evangelism makes no sense if it doesn't lead new converts into churches. I bend over backward to ensure that after my crusades, new converts will find spiritual homes.

In November 2001, Daniel Ekechukwu, a pastor in Onitsha, Nigeria, was pronounced dead at a local hospital after a disastrous accident. Hearing that Bonnke was preaching at a nearby church, Ekechukwu's wife had his body brought to the church two days after the accident.

While several pastors were guarding the body and waiting for Bonnke to finish preaching and praying in the auditorium upstairs, they noticed Ekechukwu's stomach begin to twitch. Within minutes, he had regained consciousness and was sitting up and breathing. By this time, Bonnke had left the church and gotten on a plane—unaware of the events happening in the same building.

Some have criticized Bonnke's ministry, suggesting that those who attend his crusades come only to see the miracles, but he remains undeterred by such comments. "It's wrong to go after signs and sensations, as some do," Bonnke admits. "But God has always used signs to confirm His Word."

Bonnke sat down with *Ministries Today* to answer some of these questions and to comment on the relationship of the evangelist and the local church, the future of mass crusades, and the benefits and limitations of signs and wonders in reaching the lost.

Ministries Today: When did you know that you were called to be an evangelist?

Reinhard Bonnke: Although I was called to ministry at the age of ten, it was not until 1959 when I went to Bible college that it became clear to me that Jesus had specifically directed me to become an evangelist. I knew that it was now my task for the rest of my days.

Ministries Today: How do you see your relationship to the local church and your role in partnership with it?

Bonnke: I am a church-based evangelist, because I believe that biblical evangelism makes no sense if it doesn't lead new converts into churches. I bend over backward to ensure that after my crusades, new converts will find spiritual homes. My relationship with the churches is first-class, because I say to them: "I come with my nets, and I want to borrow your boats. Together we will go out into the deep to cast the nets, catch the fish, and bring it to the shore. I will shake out every fish on the banks, and I won't take a single fish with me."

Ministries Today: How do you see the role of an evangelist complementing the other fivefold gifts?

Bonnke: I see the ministry of the evangelist as very important, but always in harmony with the rest of the fivefold ministry. When Jesus spoke about the good Samaritan, He painted a picture of Himself—the chief evangelist and the one who seeks and saves those who are lost. The parable should be an example for all evangelists to follow. We pick up those people who have fallen among thieves and are lying half-dead along the road, and we bring these people to the inn.

The inn is a picture of the church. It symbolizes the pastoral ministry. Thank God that the evangelist finds an open door so that he can bring those whom he has rescued and ensure that they will be nursed back to health, that they can become strong, and also go out to seek and save the lost.

Ministries Today: What is God looking for in an evangelist?

Bonnke: People come to me and say, "We like your passion." Passion can easily turn into fanaticism, but evangelists are not fanatical at all. I believe that an evangelist stands out when he has the compassion stirring his heart that stirred the father when the prodigal son returned. He threw his arms about his good-for-nothing, smelly son, and he kissed him. We can have the ministry of Jesus only to the degree that we have His compassion.

Ministries Today: You are a crusade evangelist. What do you believe the future is for crusade evangelism, such as yours, Billy Graham's, and that of others?

Bonnke: After World War II, some said that the days of mass evangelism were over, but with Billy Graham, they really started. There's an African proverb that says, "When sugar is mixed with sand, the elephant doesn't get it, but the ants do." Maybe my evangelism is the "elephant type," and there may be places where it will not work. Thank God for the army of witnesses, the ants, who can still extract the souls from between the sand.

Ministries Today: You've seen many dramatic miracles in your crusades. What is the role of signs and wonders in evangelism, and what are the limitations?

Bonnke: Signs and wonders are biblical, and in our crusades, they authenticate the gospel. People see it as such—especially people of other religions. At first, they may not come to listen to my preaching, but once they see how Jesus heals the sick, they open up, and they receive salvation. Sometimes I'm referred to as a "healing evangelist." I would call myself a salvation evangelist who also prays for the sick. Because sickness is not the ultimate evil, healings are not the ultimate good.

Sin is the ultimate evil. Therefore, salvation is the ultimate good. It is the greatest of all miracles. It cost God the most—His only begotten Son. Part of that is healing for the body, but this is temporal. Salvation is eternal, because our souls are immortal.

Ministries Today: When ministering in superstitious cultures, how do you keep the focus on Christ, when some would come just to see signs and wonders?

Bonnke: I've seen many witch doctors get saved in our crusades. They bring their fetishes, and we burn them in front of everybody with great rejoicing. This is a hallmark of my ministry in many places, and when you listen to those testimonies, it's absolutely fantastic. We see animists, idolaters, and people of other religions receive Christ.

Ministries Today: How do you deal with the challenge of discipling people who come to salvation in your crusades?

Bonnke: We cooperate with churches, because it is of paramount importance that converts find a spiritual home. Before we decide to go to a city, we recruit and train counselors from local churches. Sometimes we have thousands of churches cooperating. In a recent crusade we had 200,000 counselors on the field and 3.4 million people who received Jesus as their Savior. We assign new convert cards to churches based on how many counselors each church has.

Ministries Today: What will it take to evangelize the Muslim, Buddhist, and Hindu world in the twenty-first century?

Bonnke: I had a crusade last year on Easter in Khartoum, Sudan. I didn't expect too much. It was my first visit, and I knew about the situation in Sudan. The first meeting, we only had thirty thousand people. When I began to pray for the sick, the power of Jesus struck that place. A deaf mute was completely healed, and blind people received their sight.

The next night, we had 70,000, then 150,000, then 180,000, then 200,000—in the green square in the heart of Khartoum, Sudan, a Muslim country! That has given me faith for North Africa and for the hardest nations on earth.

Ministries Today: Has the American church become content financing evangelism without being involved in it?

Bonnke: Anyone who is financing evangelism is also involved in it. I preach the gospel to the poor. How could I do it if people will not financially enable me to do it? I believe that people who support my ministry participate in the eternal fruit of the ministry—those souls saved in Africa.

> I would call myself a salvation evangelist who also prays for the sick. Because sickness is not the ultimate evil, healings are not the ultimate good.

Sometimes, I think that, with so many involved with prayer and financial support, I hope that some part of the reward will be left for the preacher!

Ministries Today: What advice would you have for those who want to reach their neighbors, but are encountering a seeming lack of interest in the gospel?

Bonnke: In the parable of the sower, Jesus was the sower, and the seed was the Word. You couldn't get a better sower, and you couldn't get a better seed, but the yield depended upon the soil, and soils are different. The results are not always the same, but if we stay close to Jesus and change our methods a little bit, we will find better results. A pastor who preaches the gospel and sees some negative results shouldn't be criticized. He should be encouraged.

Ministries Today: You are a very single-minded person. How do you maintain your passion for souls?

Bonnke: It's the Holy Spirit. It grips me when I see people come to salvation. I'm a tough German, but I could cry tears when I hear the testimony of how someone gets saved. The fire I got when I was baptized in the Holy Spirit at the age of eleven keeps renewing me. We'll go on holiday when the last soul is saved. There's no way to retire now. Would you retire if you were in a rescue boat and you saw a hundred or more souls battling in the water? It's not possible, because evangelism is not a profession; it's a divine calling.

ABOUT THE AUTHOR

Matthew D. Green served for four years as editor of *Ministry Today* magazine. He is currently a freelance writer and director of communications for Pioneers, a mission agency supporting more than one hundred eighty church-planting teams among unreached people groups in eighty-two countries. His Web site may be found at www.matthewdgreen.com.

CHAPTER 17

Cell Multiplication

—M. SCOTT BOREN AND RANDALL NEIGHBOUR

SUMMARY

What is it about the DNA of a small group that makes it the optimum context for reaching the lost? Examine the evangelistic potential bound up in your living room, a Bible, and love for unbelievers.

IN HER BEST-SELLING book *Out of the Saltshaker and Into the World*, Rebecca Manley Pippert writes, "Christians and non-Christians have one thing in common: They both hate evangelism."[1] Years ago, this was the case for both of us (Randall and Scott). We reached the point where we did not want to meet a non-Christian, petrified with the thought of what God might call us to do.

In the Christian circles in which we both moved, evangelism was a strong emphasis. Although we went to different schools, we both heard pastors during our college years state, "If you don't share your faith at least once per week, you should question your salvation!" As guilty as that statement made us feel, it did not change us.

Then we both discovered a different way. In his book *Successful Home Cell Groups*, David Yonggi Cho describes how an unbelieving family was reached by the persistent expressions of love and prayer from a cell group. Upon reading the story, we both thought: *I can do that. I can be a part of a team that reaches out to the lost through acts of love and prayer.*

In most churches, small groups and evangelism are two different programs.

Small groups are for discipleship, and evangelism occurs through special events and programs. But the most effective churches that utilize cell groups define them around these two simple elements:

1. Learning about God together
2. Reaching out to the lost together

In other words, they don't separate evangelism from discipleship. These churches have redefined evangelism. The old view of evangelism sees reaching out to the lost as something an individual does to win them over to one's way of thinking so that they might be added to one's church. Like fishing with a pole, individuals cast as many lures as possible hoping for a bite, never realizing that the "hook" may actually damage many unresponsive people, pushing them further from the gospel.

NET FISHING

A different paradigm of evangelism, "net fishing," best describes the paradigm envisioned in the Gospels when Jesus said to His disciples, "I will make you fishers of men" (Matt. 4:19). They did not envision a rod, a reel, and a hook. They pictured nets, a lifestyle of spending time with other fishermen, and working together as a team each day to catch fish.

> The most effective churches that utilize cell groups define them around these two simple elements: learning about God together, and reaching out to the lost together.

Cell groups that reach the lost successfully pray often for lost friends, neighbors, family members, and co-workers. They love these people by serving them as a team and inviting them to social gatherings. As lost people see a small group sharing life and love, they experience Christ through that group. Through the new relationships and the continual prayer lifted up by their future spiritual family, they discover Christ and then make a decision to follow.

Net fishing (versus pole fishing) yields far more disciples and fewer false conversions. Why? Because unlike the individual evangelist's converts, the small group has invited the unbeliever to become part of the fellowship before they commit to Christ. A few years ago, I (Randall) received a call from a pastor in another state. He told me that a Chinese couple he knew had just moved to Houston from his area and would be open to visiting a cell group if they were invited. My cell group was having a game night later that week, so I called to invite them to come over and join us.

Not only did they come to the game night, but over the following weeks both Jing and Ling worked through the discipleship materials our group was using—even though they had not made a decision to follow Christ. My wife and I began to disciple these prebelievers as if they were new babes in Christ, and soon both Jing and Ling made public professions of faith and were baptized.

In his book *Evangelism Outside the Box*, Rick Richardson writes: "Evangelism is about helping people belong so that they come to believe. Most people today do not 'decide' to believe. In community, they 'discover' that they believe, and then they decide to affirm that publicly and to follow Christ intentionally. People are looking for a safe, accepting place to develop their identity and sense of self in community."[2]

According to Ephesians 4:12, the role of those in the fivefold ministry is "for the equipping of the saints for the work of ministry." While an evangelist will personally lead a number of people to the Lord, his or her role is actually much greater: the Ephesians 4 evangelist is an equipper of others, not just the doer of evangelism.

The equipping evangelist must go beyond the previous paradigm, which tended to confine the role of an evangelist to that of an itinerant crusade preacher. The equipping evangelist trains and empowers individuals and groups to minister to the lost through ongoing, deepening relationships by teaching them to fish with a net. In the context of a cell group, the equipping evangelist must work to establish two types of community: bonding community and bridging community.

Bonding community occurs inside the group. It strives to deepen connections between those within a group. Bridging community looks outside of itself to include others who are not part of the group. Harvard sociologist Robert Putnam writes, "Bonding social capital constitutes a kind of sociological superglue, whereas bridging social capital provides a sociological WD-40."[3] Bonding and bridging community work together to reach people for Christ.

BONDING COMMUNITY

It has been said many times that the church needs to get outside its walls and reach out to the world. With such beliefs as a premise, the church has developed enough evangelism strategies to fill up a university library. Whether it was "each one reach one," "lighthouse prayer," "ecumenical crusades," or a "small group campaign," the church always has a plan to get people outside the walls.

In John 17:21, Jesus prayed for the church that we would be one with one another as Jesus and the Father are one. Then He states the purpose of this unity with one another: so that the world might know that Jesus was sent by the Father. If we take this prayer to heart, His evangelism strategy begins first inside the four walls of the church itself, with bonding community.

Too many churches are going outside the walls when what is happening inside the walls is not worth the cost of a printed invitation. Outsiders look at the church and fail to see a way of life that is different from their own. Divorce rates are just as high inside the church. Church members are often just as materialistic, work just as much overtime, compromise their morals, and are often just as depressed and downtrodden as the rest of the world.

Through the eyes of the unchurched, the only difference is that church-goers attend a weekly service, listen to a sermon, give away money, and try to live morally upright lives. Jesus said, "By this all will know that you are My disciples, if you have love for one another" (John 13:35). Most churches need much more than a new evangelism program that will help them develop bridging community. They need to establish bonding communities so that they will have something attractive to offer those outside the church.

Cell groups specialize in developing this bonding community. They provide a place where people can share their struggles, pray for one another, and see personal transformation. Such practices establish a strong bond between members, which stands in contrast to the way the world operates.

BRIDGING COMMUNITY

Research has consistently revealed that between 80 and 90 percent of all the people in churches today were led to the Lord by a friend, neighbor, co-worker, or family member. Bridging community is about becoming friends with people, loving those who are close, and then helping them discover Christ in the midst of a new Christian family.

When a group breaks through to bonding community, the members are surprised by how good it feels. Typically, a protective mechanism from the flesh rises up, and group members want to hoard that which God has given. The flesh yearns to turn inward and raise walls. Bonding can become so strong in a small group of Christians that a desire to cocoon becomes the purpose for its very existence.

This protection often comes in the form of making outsiders feel unwelcome. Group members use words and phrases that are foreign to outsiders such as *sanctification, justification,* or *washed in the blood.* Sometimes, they pray loudly and quote Scripture as if it were a weapon formed to hurt. Outsiders rarely feel comfortable in this environment, and they don't stick around.

> Too many churches are going outside the walls when what is happening inside the walls is not worth the cost of a printed invitation.

Without the help of the evangelist to equip the group to develop bridging community, a local church's small groups will get stuck being a religious club. Effective groups must be coached to consider the lost as more important than themselves and to receive the stranger without the expectation that they will change.

When bridging has been taught and embraced by the group, many different outreach strategies will work. We don't have to cajole people into accepting Christ's love. We only need to allow them to experience our God-given joy and join us.

Cell-group leaders and members need more evangelists within local churches who understand that their roles are to equip the saints to live in both bonding and bridging community. To fulfill the Great Commission, evangelism must become more than a leadership role or a program in which only a handful of members feel gifted enough to participate.

ABOUT THE AUTHORS

The author of *Making Cell Groups Work*, M. Scott Boren serves on staff at Hosanna! Church in Houston. Randall G. Neighbour is the president of TOUCH Outreach Ministries (www.touchusa.org) and author of several books, including *Community Life 101.*

FOR FURTHER STUDY

M. Scott Boren, *Making Cell Groups Work: Navigating the Transformation to a Cell-Based Church*

Joel Comiskey, *How to Lead a Great Cell Group Meeting…So People Want to Come Back*

David Yonggi Cho, *Successful Home Cell Groups*

CHAPTER 18

Future Pastor

—TOMMY BARNETT

SUMMARY

One of America's best-loved pastors shares his secret for staying relevant: risk reinventing yourself.

IT'S BEEN SAID that the pastor today is more of a CEO than a shepherd, but perhaps there is a better metaphor to describe the twenty-first-century pastor.

As a church grows and broadens its ministry, the pastor must begin to view his role not only as a shepherd but also as a rancher. As a church expands its reach to meet the needs of different groups of people, the senior pastor must be willing to allow others to shepherd those distinct groups. As a rancher, he helps set the direction for all these shepherds so the entire flock can embrace a like vision and operate in unity.

In order for a church to reach its community today, one must be willing to explore innovative ways to communicate to people who are receiving information, inspiration, and motivation differently than they did just a few years ago.

Each year, when thousands of pastors and leaders gather at our Pastor's School, we emphasize that the method is not sacred—the message is. As long as we maintain the integrity of the good news of Christ, we can be—and we must be—innovative in the way we present the message so that it is relevant to people's lives.

Ultimately, there are two priorities set before the pastor as his holy charge. They are eternal and must be at the forefront of what he does: the Word of God and people. Everything else will pass away, but the Word of God will remain. And an emphasis on people and their everlasting souls will help keep the pastor focused and limit distractions such as buildings and programs, which—albeit important—must not become the main focus in ministry.

If the pastor, or a rancher, if you will, has these priorities in mind and heart, it will be easier for him to reach the community with new methods, but with the same message of the love of God.

Numerous studies have shown that one of the primary barriers to churches reaching unchurched people in their communities is that many people feel churches are not relevant to their lives.

I have always felt that the church should be on the cutting edge in the ways that it reaches out to people. Fifty years ago, using props and dramatic presentations while presenting illustrated sermons was considered practically heretical. Realizing that our society is becoming more and more visually oriented and less literary, we have to bring the message of Christ to people in a manner that makes sense to them.

> Numerous studies have shown that one of the primary barriers to churches reaching unchurched people in their communities is that many people feel churches are not relevant to their lives.

Similarly, when we removed the hymnals from the pews at Phoenix First and replaced them with two large projection screens, many thought that a sacred element of worship had been replaced by some sterile technology. Instead, the worship experience has been enhanced with the use of technology that makes the message relevant to people.

A pastor must examine the church and its ministries, its facilities, and, ultimately, himself to see that the love of God is being effectively communicated to people in a way that makes sense in the postmodern context.

A pastor should be willing to risk utilizing cultural innovations in order to spread the gospel. For example, we often capitalize on the marketing efforts that are capturing the attention of millions of people in order for those same people to hear our message.

We recently advertised an illustrated sermon titled "American Idols," complete with a vocal contest, and unchurched people from all over the community came. When the message was presented that idolatry and the pursuit of fame leaves people with a hollow emptiness that only Jesus Christ can fill, more than one thousand people came to the altars to give their hearts to the Lord.

We've built new high-tech buildings for youth and children, a "Youth Walk" hangout for teens, and a cafe in order to create an environment where we can reach the next generation. Young people who might not otherwise come to church are affected by the message to such an extent that many of them don't want services to end as they continue to seek the Lord.

If the pastor is a CEO, as some church leadership experts claim, then perhaps some *reinventing*—as the corporate world would call it—is in order. When companies reinvent, they strengthen their identities and visions while increasing the scope of their outreach.

Without compromising the enduring values of salvation, healing, the Holy Spirit, and the Second Coming, we must create innovative means of communicating these truths to a generation that is biblically illiterate.

One of the ways that we as pastors can examine our churches' relevance in our communities is to see if our churches represent the people that we are trying to reach in our weekly attendance. If not, we must be willing to take the risk of reinventing ourselves in order to reach a lost and dying world for Christ.

ABOUT THE AUTHOR

A veteran of more than fifty years of ministry, Tommy Barnett is the pastor of Phoenix First Assembly, an innovative congregation he has served for twenty-four years. Barnett is the author of several books, including *Hidden Power, Dream Again*, and *Adventure Yourself.*

FOR FURTHER STUDY

Tommy Barnett, *There's a Miracle in Your House*

Tommy Barnett, *Adventure Yourself*

Tommy Barnett, *Reaching Your Dreams: 7 Steps For Turning Dreams Into Reality*

CHAPTER 19

Tommy Barnett: Dream Weaver

—MATTHEW GREEN

SUMMARY

After fifty years of ministry, Tommy Barnett is still thinking big—and squeezing every last drop out of life.

T OMMY BARNETT IS running out of time. "I'm dying while I'm preaching," the pastor of Phoenix First Assembly tells his congregation at a recent Sunday morning service. "I'm going to take my life and squeeze it like a washrag—squeeze every last drop out of it for the glory of God."

Don't let the seemingly somber words fool you. Barnett, who celebrates fifty years of ministry this October, is just as optimistic and energetic as he's always been—maybe more so. But these days there's an urgency about him that's hard to ignore.

"As you get older, you realize that what you're going to do, you need to do now," he told *Ministries Today* in a recent interview. "Imagine if one day I drove by this church and thought to myself: *What if I'd given it my best? What if I'd given my money or my time or sacrificed some things to make it the focus of my life?*"

Instead, Barnett says he's "cranked it up" even more since he turned fifty years old—cutting out vacation days to help his son Matthew at the Dream Center in Los Angeles and turning in his country club membership. "They

131

don't mow the grass where I hit the ball, anyway," he adds.

And he's seen dramatic results, particularly in the last four years. "Blessings are overtaking me," Barnett says with a bewildered smile. "More money has come through these hands for the work of the Lord; I've seen more people saved, more miracles, and more signs and wonders than in the previous forty-six years."

CHANGING METHODS

After a quick ride around the church campus in one of its covered golf carts, one would assume that the mastermind behind it all would be a little younger—a little more radical than the wiry sixty-six-year-old who says his preaching is the same as it was when he started fifty years ago.

A building dedicated to youth ministry boasts a high-tech auditorium, a gymnasium, and a Starbucks—the first church-based franchise in the United States.

The newly opened children's ministry pavilion features glass walls that can be retracted like garage doors to expand seating into an outdoor amphitheater.

Halfway up the rocky mountainside behind the church, ground is being broken for a prayer chapel and gardens.

While he still describes his sermons as a "greasy wrench" rather than a "masterpiece" ("I'm not preaching to impress. I'm preaching to fix something in our lives."), Barnett has refocused other areas of his ministry to adapt to changing times.

"I used to be very, very regimented," he says sheepishly. "Hymns only, ties and suits, no applauding in the church." He can't put his finger on it, but Barnett admits that over the years, something shifted.

"I'm more open to change than I've ever been in my life," he says. "I'm going to do whatever it takes—if it's in good taste—to reach people."

Barnett recalls being one of the first pastors to trade in hymnals for projection screens and high-tech gadgetry. "The preacher's responsible for this change," he says. And while many pastors would resort to cajoling to bring their congregations into the twenty-first century, Barnett used a different approach:

"'We like the old hymns, and we'll still use them,' I told the church. 'But let's quit being selfish. We've been singing these songs all our lives—they were once new to us. I'm tired of them. I want to rock 'n' roll a little bit.'"

And rock they do. Even in the early Sunday service supposedly populated by the more "mature" members of Phoenix First, gray-headed worshipers sway and clap to the music as the teens in the Masters Commission choir belt out upbeat praise choruses.

Members aren't the only ones taking notice these days. Recently, *Phoenix Magazine* rated the church one of the top ten hottest places to be on a Sunday night.

"I've made up my mind; I'm going to be relevant," Barnett says firmly. "The method's not sacred, but the message sure is."

UNCHANGED MESSAGE

Barnett's message is—and always has been—about reaching the lost. "We need to be soul-winning," he says. "If we don't watch it, we'll just become an entertaining place where we shout and sing and make people feel good."

While he has no problem with the seeker-sensitive church model, Barnett is concerned that some pastors may be putting on a good show but "flaking out" when it comes time for an altar call. "I don't want people to have a false salvation," he says. "Drifting into church, enjoying the fellowship and music, but never having a conversion experience."

Barnett suggests that current signs of growth in the church could be nothing more than what he calls a "Constantine revival"—numerically large, but not built on genuine conversions.

> I'm more open to change than I've ever been in my life. I'm going to do whatever it takes—if it's in good taste—to reach people.

Barnett's passion for souls reaches back to the sixteen years he traveled as an evangelist before becoming pastor of Westside Assembly of God in Davenport, Iowa—a church he grew from seventy-four to forty-four hundred before he came to Phoenix First twenty-five years ago.

"I can win more souls as a pastor than I could as an evangelist," Barnett says, "because I have a core of people around me to help."

DREAM RECRUITS

This is the challenge he shares with the seven thousand pastors who attend his annual Pastor's School: get a vision to reach the lost, and gather a group of dreamers around you to carry out the vision.

All but one of Barnett's staff came from within the church. "Most were businessmen who had a heart for God," he says. "I watched to see if they were the ones who came to the altar, served people, loved people."

While most would argue that Barnett has recruited some very gifted leaders to serve on his staff, talent is one of the last qualities on his checklist. "I look for loyal, positive people who love God," he says. "They may not be the most talented, but they have character."

Barnett's staff reflects his upbeat outlook on life and ministry, but he suspects that they have more potential for success than he did early in his own ministry. "Most of them have a better education than me, and they know how to use computers and technology," he says. "They're going to be able to go further than me, because they are a product of what they've seen and heard."

"We are a permission-giving church," Barnett says. "I want people to become great." As a result of this philosophy of releasing rather than closely guarding church ministries, many have outgrown the confines of Phoenix First and become national ministries—Athletes International, National Association of Marriage Enhancement (NAME), and Master's Commission, to name a few.

"A lot of pastors may feel threatened when a great ministry rises up in their church," Barnett says. "My joy is seeing these ministries become great—I live a vicarious life."

"A LIST OF DON'TS"

More than what he has done, Barnett credits his success to what he hasn't done. "Don't just have a 'to do' list," he tells his congregation. "Have a 'don't do' list, as well. Knowing what is your business and what's not your business is the secret to an effective life."

In an age when some pastors' kids get more space on the police blotter than the honor roll, Barnett made it his business to put his family first. As a result, both of his sons, Luke and Matthew, are in full-time pastoral ministry, and his daughter, Kristie, and her husband are faithful members of Phoenix First.

Barnett admits that there are people who have reached the world but lost their children. "But what about those who have reached the world and not lost their children?" he asks. "It is possible if you keep your priorities straight and include your family in the ministry."

"My kids always wanted to go to church," Barnett says. "It was never a question. They were there on Sunday morning, Sunday night, and Wednesday night. But they knew that the rest of the week we were going to do things together. We played night and day when we weren't in church."

This doesn't mean that the family hasn't made significant sacrifices. Barnett recalls the Christmas morning when they were preparing to exchange gifts, and the phone rang with news that a church member had been in a car accident and was dying in the hospital.

"The kids were anticipating opening presents, but I said, 'Please understand that this is important. I'll be back.' They all said, 'OK, Daddy,' because our priorities were in the right place."

Some pastors argue that priorities should be arranged with God first, family second, and ministry last, but Barnett sees it a different way.

"I say we put God-dash-people as the highest priority," he argues. "Jesus said that the only way you can feed, clothe, or minister to Him is when you feed, clothe, and minister to others."

A people-centered ministry has grown Phoenix First to a church of fifteen thousand, but does Barnett ever want to get away from it all and trade his pulpit for a desk job?

> We need to be soul-winning. If we don't watch it, we'll just become an entertaining place where we shout and sing and make people feel good.

"Every Monday morning I want to resign," he says with a smile. "But before I resign, I say, 'Lord, I'm going to have a cup of Starbucks coffee'—there are some mornings I have two. After the second cup, I'm ready to work one more week."

One would never imagine that the favorite pastime of a man who's made a life of caring for people is—of all things—spending time alone.

"If you love people you must spend time alone, alone with God studying and meditating," Barnett says. "Every time you go back before the people, they have to know that you've been with God."

With the same effort he expends in making time for himself, Barnett labors to keep his connection to the people in his care, sometimes staying for hours after church services to give hugs, prayers, and encouragement.

"Everyone in this church would probably say, 'Yeah, Pastor's my friend,'" Barnett says. "But I also have people in this church who've never shaken my hand, because they want me to be free to minister to new people."

"I do things to keep me loving people," he says, describing times he's driven into the projects as well as into the neighborhoods of lonely millionaires.

"Even more than my message, they need to know that I love them," Barnett says. "And I need their love, too!"

ABOUT THE AUTHOR

Matthew D. Green served for four years as editor of *Ministry Today* magazine. He is currently a freelance writer and director of communications for Pioneers, a mission agency supporting more than one hundred eighty church-planting teams among unreached people groups in eighty-two countries. His Web site may be found at www.matthewdgreen.com.

FOR FURTHER STUDY

Tommy Barnett, *Reaching Your Dreams*

Tommy Barnett, *Hidden Power: Tap into a Kingdom Principle That Will Change You Forever*

Tommy Barnett, *Multiplication: Unlock the Biblical Factors to Multiply Your Effectiveness in Leadership & Ministry*

CHAPTER 20

Thugs in the Pulpit

—RICHARD DOBBINS

SUMMARY

Why are so many pastors abusing the trust of those God has placed in their care? Here are the warning signs—and the road to healing for sheep wounded by the shepherd.

F
EW LEADERS IN our society have more power over others than ministers—power to abuse or power to set free. However, people are more likely to have a healthy wariness of "quacks" in law, medicine, and counseling than they do of "quacks" in religion. Although most pastors are both gifted and godly, many Christians are naïve enough to assume that any man or woman who is able to build a congregation is healthy. It is such naïveté that makes people vulnerable to unscrupulous pastors.

People don't realize the far-reaching effects their pastors will have on them and their families. Consequently, they exercise more care in finding competent physicians to care for their bodies than they do in choosing competent pastors to help them care for their souls. How do abusive ministers get this kind of control over people? The roots of this awesome clerical power deserve some examination. They are biblical, social, institutional, and personal.

BIBLICAL

In his three pastoral epistles, Paul stresses the importance of confining this power to healthy pastors. Then he instructs believers to give special honor to healthy pastors who preach and teach well. (See 1 Timothy 5:17.)

But Paul also acknowledges that pastors may fall into sin or become abusive, so he gives specific directions for bringing accusations against elders. (See 1 Timothy 5:19.) However, abusive pastors sometimes counter any efforts to hold them accountable for their actions by misusing biblical passages such as, "'Do not touch My anointed ones, and do My prophets no harm" (1 Chron. 16:22).

SOCIAL

The Constitution of the United States guarantees religious freedom. This secures the pastor's right to preach and teach whatever he or she chooses. The government also empowers ministers to marry and bury people. In spite of the media attention to some ministers' scandalous sins, the pastor is still the most highly trusted person in the community.

INSTITUTIONAL

The institutional church enhances the power of the pastor through the credentialing process. Unfortunately, few religious credentialing bodies take any precautionary measures to protect the public from abusive personalities attempting to enter the ministry. Even those who do limit their screening to personal references and interviews.

The growing number of independent churches put even fewer checks in place when credentialing people. Since independent churches are accountable to no other body of authority, the risk of pastoral abuse tends to be higher among them.

PERSONAL

Most people implicitly trust their pastors. They do not look at their pastors with the same discretion or suspicion that protects them from other harmful people in their communities. This enhances the pastors' power and gives them greater opportunity than any other civic leader to hurt or help people.

DIFFERING DEGREES

Abusive pastors have an uncanny ability to pick their victims. They usually choose people who are unsuspecting and somewhat naïve—people who cannot find it in their hearts to question one who says he is "a man of God."

Abusive pastors also carefully select the leaders for their congregations. They choose men and women who are willing to give total and unquestioned allegiance to the pastor in return for positions of prominence and power in the church. These leaders become the abusive pastor's agents for controlling and manipulating the congregation. The degrees of pastoral abuse may be viewed on a continuum ranging from financial abuse to sexual abuse with diminished personhood in between.

Financial abuse

Abusive pastors may manipulate wealthy contributors into making major donations or investing in schemes that will financially benefit themselves. Or, the pastors may borrow from parishioners and fail to repay them. Perhaps the most devastating cases of financial abuse involve pastors who directly persuade people or allow their names to be used to encourage people to invest money in pyramid schemes or other highly questionable business ventures. Wise pastors know that if an investment scheme seems too good to be true, it probably is.

An even more despicable form of financial abuse is deceiving people to believe that a miraculous covenantal offering to the minister will bring to them an exponentially larger amount of money than they gave. This kind of clergy quackery is often seen on late-night television in markets where there are viewers desperate enough for money to make this a profitable venture for religious hucksters. Those who engage in this kind of religious racketeering are a disgrace to the ministry.

Diminished personhood

In the last thirty-five years I have seen many victims of pastoral abuse who are left with little or no sense of personal worth and suffer from depression and anxiety. They have lost faith in everything and everybody.

Simply establishing rapport with these people is a difficult therapeutic challenge. So just getting them to feel safe enough to open up and tell their stories is our first goal. Verbally processing feelings that have been bottled up for months or years brings relief to them.

These stories often involve accounts of abusive pastors planting seeds of suspicion among members of the same family. A wife is told that her husband doesn't really care for her as the pastor does. And a husband is convinced that he can't trust his wife.

An abusive pastor is sinister enough to make each member of his church feel they have a unique relationship with him or her, and that other members are envious and jealous of that relationship. Eventually, each person feels closely linked to the pastor but suspicious of the group. The only link they have with one another is through the pastor.

Coming out of such sick personality cults is a gigantic step for people because they have been taught that if they ever say anything critical about the pastor, God will severely judge them or something dreadful will happen to them or their children.

Sexual abuse

Typically, sexual abuse begins with the pastor's subtle calculated touch that obviously violates personal boundaries. In reflecting on what has happened, the person is confused about the intentions of it. After all, this was their pastor who touched them. They do not want to feel it was intentional. In their mind, the pastor would never do anything like that.

> Abusive pastors have an uncanny ability to pick their victims. They usually choose people who are unsuspecting and somewhat naïve.

Often, this violation occurs in the context of counseling or comforting a member in crisis. So the person assumes that the pastor just got carried away in his efforts to help.

However, when no objection is raised, the abusive pastor seeks the next opportunity to cross a more intimate boundary. Once the sexual intent is obvious, the person feels compromised, but may feel that they were responsible for inviting the advance in some way.

The pastor then persuades the person that it is in everyone's interests to keep what has happened confidential. After all, what would happen to the church, to the person's family, and to the pastor and his family if this were to be revealed?

How do people get trapped into such abusive groups? Usually they stumble across the groups through the misguided sincerity of their own spiritual search. Or they have been craftily recruited by members of the groups.

HEALING THE WOUNDED

1. Create a loving, accepting environment where the person can learn to trust again.

The longer the person has been deceived and the deeper they have been hurt, the more difficult it will be for that person to trust you. Help him or her trust again by giving unconditional love and acceptance.

2. Let them tell their stories.

When people are breaking free from an abusive leader, they are torn by powerful, conflicting emotions. They feel violated, betrayed, and duped. They are angry and outraged, but they may be too fearful or too guilty to get in touch with those feelings at first.

As they tell their stories, they discover that guilt is not an appropriate response to their abuse, and the love of Christ helps them overcome their fears (1 John 4:18). Then they are ready to deal with their anger and outrage.

3. Set realistic expectations for recovery.

Even through prayer and godly counseling, recovery usually requires from six to eighteen months and will follow four predictable stages: First, shock—"This is like a nightmare; I can't believe it is true." (This stage lasts from a few hours to a few days.) Second, storm—intense emotional conflict and deep depression. (This stage lasts from several weeks to several months.) Third, search—"Where is God in all of this? How can I make sense of it?" (This stage lasts for several months.) Finally, sequel—peace and joy emerge again.

While accompanying people through this painful process, I try to help them learn to distinguish the difference between a healthy spiritual experience and an unhealthy one. A careful search of the New Testament reveals the characteristics of a church that encourages such spiritual health:

- **Is affirmed in fellowship.** People need to beware of religious groups whose conformity to rigid legalistic practices and strange beliefs cut them off from other Christians.

- **Sees God as love.** Abusive churches control people with guilt, fear, shame, and a suspicion of other churches who have not found the "true way."

- **Teaches the believer that being unworthy does not mean that we are worthless.** Our self-worth was established at Calvary. (See 1 Peter

1:18–19; 1 Corinthians 6:19–20.) We are not worthy of the price Christ paid for our redemption, but the fact that He paid it assures us that we are not worthless.

Along with the above, a healthy church helps one deal with reality—not deny it; is not rigid, but flexible enough to help one deal with the changes of the future; helps one deal with stress and anxiety; helps one manage anger constructively; balances work and play; and helps one love and forgive others.

LOOKING INSIDE

How do we as spiritual leaders identify traits in ourselves that may lead to spiritual abuse? Here is a list of indications that you may have abusive tendencies:

- I have a grandiose sense of self-importance and tend to exaggerate my talents and achievements.

- I am preoccupied with fantasies of unlimited success.

- I see myself as someone "special" who can only be understood by other "special" or high-status people.

- I require excessive admiration and feel entitled to special treatment.

- Others are expected to automatically comply with my expectations.

- I take advantage of others to achieve my own goals.

- I lack compassion and am unwilling to identify with the feelings and needs of others.

- I am arrogant and haughty.

- I am preoccupied with unjustified doubts about the loyalty or trustworthiness of friends and associates.

- I fear confiding in people since they may maliciously use any information I give them to do me harm.

- I read demeaning or threatening meanings into innocent remarks.

- I bear grudges and am unforgiving of others I feel have harmed me.

- I am quick to perceive attacks on my character or reputation that are not apparent to others, and I react angrily or counterattack.

- I am deceitful and seduce others for my own profit or pleasure.

- I am impulsive in my actions and fail to plan ahead.

- I may be excessively devoted to work to the exclusion of leisure activities and friendships.

- I am inflexible, stubborn, and controlling, insisting that others submit exactly to my way of doing things.

- I unreasonably criticize and scorn other ministers and people in positions of authority in the church.

- I am uncomfortable in situations where I am not the center of attention.

- I believe I am doing a much better job than others think I am doing.

Each of us needs to engage in the kind of conscientious, ongoing self-examination that will keep us sensitive to the slightest indication of any characteristics of spiritual abuse in our own ministries. If you recognize a number of these traits in your ministry, reach out for help.

The abuse of pastoral power is a treatable, but not self-correcting problem. However, by humbling yourself and submitting to a godly counselor, these character traits can be conquered.

The pastoral power God has given you does not need to be abusive. It can be expressed in ways to set people free to be the people God has called them to be. Everyone in the ministry has an obligation to God and to the public to identify ministers who abuse their spiritual power, confront them, and attempt to get them the help they obviously need.

This confrontation should be undertaken in a loving and biblical manner (Matt. 18:15–17). My experience indicates that few abusive pastors respond positively to such attempts to help them address these issues in their lives, but they deserve the opportunity. Many of them are very gifted individuals whose ministries could bring great healing and freedom to God's people.

ABOUT THE AUTHOR

Richard D. Dobbins, PhD, is a Christian psychologist and minister. After twenty-six years of pastoral experience, Dobbins launched EMERGE Ministries, a Christian mental health center in Akron, Ohio.

FOR FURTHER STUDY

Richard D. Dobbins, *Invisible Imprint: What Others Feel When in Your Presence*

Richard D. Dobbins, *Your Spiritual and Emotional Power*

Marc Dupont, *Toxic Churches: Restoration from Spiritual Abuse*

Mike Fehlauer, *Exposing Spiritual Abuse: How to Rediscover God's Love When the Church Has Let You Down*

Ken Blue, *Healing Spiritual Abuse: How to Break Free From Bad Church Experiences*

George Bloomer, *Authority Abusers: Breaking Free From Spiritual Abuse*

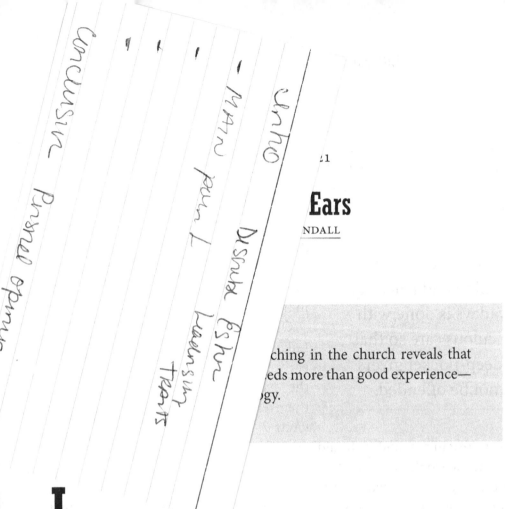

Conclusion Pursual opinion

Intro

Main point 1

Disprove false humanism Traits

41

Ears

NDALL

ching in the church reveals that
eds more than good experience—
gy.

IS SOUND TEACHING primary today, or are teachers merely scratching the itching ears of their hearers? It depends where you look. In some reformed or mainline denominational churches, teaching is likely primary. The problem with most of them is that they are overfed. (I speak as a reformed theologian and pastor.)

They remind me of fat sheep that keep eating more and more and need to be poked to let air out before they die of eating too much. To quote my predecessor at Westminster Chapel, Dr. Martyn Lloyd-Jones, they are "perfectly orthodox and perfectly useless."

But if you look to Charismatic and Pentecostal churches—those who fancy themselves "Spirit-filled"—you will find the opposite. Teaching is not primary. Worship, signs and wonders, and an obsession with the benefits of giving and receiving are the cornerstones of what passes for solid teaching.

Instead of an emphasis upon the real reason Jesus died—the cross, the Resurrection, knowing Christ—teaching has become largely concerned with answering the question, "What will this do for me?" This is the very reason

145

"revival tarries," to use the late Leonard Ravenhill's phrase.

Is the place of teaching in our churches given the same profile as in the New Testament? Not in the least.

The writings of the apostle Paul comprise two-thirds of the New Testament—almost entirely teaching. Consider the four Gospels, which are composed of the parables and the sermons of Jesus. They are all teaching. Look at the Book of Acts.

> Much that passes for preaching and teaching nowadays is done with meticulous care so that the deep-pocket givers will not be offended.

The key issues were the reason Jesus died and rose from the dead, the relationship of circumcision to salvation, the offense of the cross—all interlaced with persecution in the early church over teaching.

One of the forgotten observations of Luke is the way he initially described the early church immediately after recording the event of Pentecost: "They devoted themselves to the apostles' teaching" (Acts 2:42, NIV). Teaching came first in the New Testament, and it should come first today.

Instead, it would seem that much that passes for preaching and teaching nowadays is done with meticulous care so that the deep-pocket givers will not be offended. Teachers are more concerned with filtering the content through the minds of hearers than they are with confronting the lost who are going to hell.

By the way, when is the last time you actually heard an authentic, heartfelt sermon devoted entirely to the teaching of eternal punishment? Is there a hint of the appetite of the church today if one judges this by the preaching on Christian television these days?

While some Christians might crave healthier fare, you'd never know it to watch the average "teaching" program. Instead of solid, sound teaching that reflects the God of the Bible, we hear of the preacher's desire to make people write in (with a generous contribution) at the end of the program.

But when contributions are needed to keep these preachers on the air, one wonders if they end up "playing to the gallery" and "ringing certain bells" to keep the money flowing in.

If I am asked what some of the false teachings are that have invaded the church today, I would answer:

- The dilution of the New Testament teaching on eternal punishment

- An absence of emphasis on the Holy Spirit's role in convicting of sin, righteousness, and judgment before people can be saved

- Ignorance of the primary reason Jesus died and rose from the dead— for our salvation, not for our healing and prosperity

- An overemphasis on what appeals to one's personal comfort to motivate to obedience rather than being motivated by the glory of God alone

These and other issues should be addressed by the teachers God has given the church. But it would appear that the gift of teaching has fallen on hard times in the body of Christ today.

ISN'T THE HOLY SPIRIT ENOUGH?

The office of the teacher is the last on the list of those offices, or special anointings, given in Ephesians 4:11. It is the least controversial, but possibly the most neglected and needed of the five. The Greek word for "teacher" (*didaskalos*) is found in the New Testament fifty-eight times. It was a common way the twelve addressed Jesus—"Master" in the King James Version—which appears in the four Gospels alone at least forty-five times. The Greek word *didasko* ("to teach") is found ninety-five times in the New Testament, and *didakee* ("teaching") appears thirty times in the New Testament.

In the ancient Hellenistic world these words taken together referred to instruction and were used to denote the insight of the one to be instructed and the knowledge presupposed in the teacher. The example, not merely the instruction of the teacher, formed a bridge to the knowledge and the ability of the pupil. Teaching referred to the inspiration of practical and theoretical knowledge.

There was a deep connection between the content of instruction and the example of the teacher, since the teacher would often be imitated by the pupil. One thus recalls Paul's final word to Timothy, "You, however, know all about my teaching, my way of life, my purpose, faith, patience, love, endurance" (2 Tim. 3:10, NIV). Doctrine and manner of life were intimately related.

Is it true that if people are soundly converted they will progress in their walks with Christ simply because they have the Holy Spirit to guide and teach them? Most of Paul's letters—two-thirds of the New Testament—plus Hebrews, all underline the premise that the Holy Spirit is not enough! If the Holy Spirit were enough, then one would just learn from Him and drink at the fountain of His peace—and never need to open the Bible.

But God gave us the Bible—the Holy Spirit's greatest product—that we might know the Spirit's mind. We need to be filled with the Spirit again and again and again. What happened at Pentecost in Acts 2 was virtually repeated in Acts 4:31 and following, and this must happen to us. It is then that we will grasp the teaching of the New Testament at a level rarely experienced. Never forget: the Holy Spirit wrote the Bible, and if we are to understand it, we must be on good terms with Him.

In fact, the role of the Holy Spirit is to bring to our minds what has been previously taught. If sound teaching is not in our minds in the first place, there is nothing for the Holy Spirit to remind us of. (See John 14:26.)

TEACHING AND THE FIVEFOLD MINISTRY

The fivefold ministry depicted in Ephesians 4:11 shows not only the "givenness" and diversity of leadership in the earliest church but also the order in which the ministry functioned and generally unfolded.

> If sound teaching is not in our minds in the first place, there is nothing for the Holy Spirit to remind us of.

First came the apostles who had authority to lay both doctrinal foundations and validate that authority partly through signs and wonders.

The prophetic ministry gave immediate direction and guidance for Christians, especially at a time when there was no New Testament to consult. This does not negate the need for the prophetic today, but one cannot help but wonder if people are more interested in the prophetic word than the written or preached Word—even though we have the Bible at our fingertips.

Evangelists, the bearers of good news, could describe the role of virtually every Christian in ancient times although there emerged a special gifting in this area. All Christians have the gift of spreading the gospel within them, and this is a gold mine that is largely unexplored in the church at the present time.

The role of the pastor quickly surfaced, since all God's sheep need leadership, loving care, and sometimes discipline.

The teacher can possibly be said to describe the apostle and pastor but refers mainly to the ongoing upholding of apostolic doctrine so that all the body of Christ could be aptly instructed and well informed as to what they should believe.

Some pastors are not strong teachers or preachers, and some teachers and preachers are not good pastors. But sound teaching is needed in the body of Christ. This way a believer's faith will be strong and their discernment sharp when it is necessary to detect false teaching.

There is a distinction between the teacher and the preacher. Preaching refers to the message as well as method but largely embraces exhortation and evangelism. In a sense, preaching can be done by any believer, whereas the teacher is gifted with knowledge and the ability to impart knowledge. Paul, John, and Jude, in particular, had to deal with false teaching that crept into the church toward the end of the first century—largely Gnosticism and the teaching of the Judaizers (Jews who made professions of faith but who probably were never truly converted by the Holy Spirit).

CONTENDING FOR THE FAITH

The little epistle of Jude indicates that the writer had hoped to write a soteriological treatise, but due to the onslaught of false doctrine that came from counterfeit ministers, he warned that we must earnestly contend for the faith "once for all" entrusted to the saints (Jude 3).

The "once for all" refers to a body of doctrine that needed to be understood and upheld. This shows that we are not to teach just anything we like; we are duty-bound to uphold holy Scripture and that faith "once for all" delivered to the church. This is one of the reasons we still need the office of the teacher.

I believe that every Christian is called to be a theologian. Most believers today could not tell you what they believe or why. How many do you know who can explain the doctrine of justification by faith—which turned the world upside down in the sixteenth century? But Paul said that Jesus was raised for our justification (Rom. 4:25).

Worse still, how many Christians could be prepared in ten seconds to lead a lost person to a saving knowledge of Christ? It takes not only a good experience but also—sooner or later—good theology to do this. The role of the teacher is therefore not merely an option; it is urgently needed—now more than ever.

ABOUT THE AUTHOR

R. T. Kendall was the pastor of Westminster Chapel in London for twenty-five years. Educated at Southern Baptist Theological Seminary and Oxford University, Kendall is the author of more than thirty books, including the bestseller *Total Forgiveness*. He lives with his wife, Louise, in Key Largo, Florida.

FOR FURTHER STUDY

R. T. Kendall, *The Anointing: Yesterday, Today, Tomorrow*

R. T. Kendall, *Understanding Theology: The Means of Developing a Healthy Church in the Twenty-first Century*

R. T. Kendall, *In Pursuit of His Glory: My 25 Years at Westminster Chapel*

CHAPTER 22

Word + Spirit = Power

—R. T. KENDALL

SUMMARY

A divorce of the Word and the Spirit in the church has resulted in "fast-food" teaching and preaching—often tasty, but seldom healthful.

THERE'S BEEN A silent divorce in the church—not between a man and a woman, but between the Word of God and the Spirit of God. As with any divorce, sometimes the children stay with the mother, and sometimes they stay with the father. In this divorce, some have embraced the Spirit, and others the Word. However, I believe that our teaching and preaching will only be effective if they are firmly grounded in the Word of God and entirely saturated with the Spirit of God.

What is the difference? Those on the "Word" side emphasize sound doctrine, expository preaching, contending for the faith. "We need to get back to the teaching of the Reformation," they say, "to rediscover the doctrine of justification by faith, the sovereignty of God, and to know the God of Jonathan Edwards."

Those on the "Spirit" side emphasize the prophetic word, signs, wonders, miracles, and the power demonstrated in the Book of Acts. "Until we see that dimension of the Spirit that is seen in the early church—with all the gifts of the Spirit in operation—the honor of God's name will not be restored, nor will the world take any real notice of the church," these people say.

It is not one or the other that is needed, but both. This simultaneous combination will result in spontaneous combustion. It is only then that the revival for which we pray and another Great Awakening, which is sorely needed, will take place.

VALUING THE WORD

In the Old Testament, God has revealed Himself in essentially two ways: His Word and His name. His Word is the infallible expression of who He is and what He declares to be true. His Word is His integrity put on the line. His name reveals His identity, His power, and His reputation.

When I teach, I sometimes ask people to vote for which, in their opinion, is the more important of the two to God Himself: His Word or His name? In my experience, most people believe that God's name is more important to Him than His Word. The answer is actually provided by David in Psalm 138:2: "Thou hast magnified thy word above all thy name" (KJV).

Why? First, His Word came prior to the disclosure of His name. It was His Word that spoke Creation into existence (Gen. 1:3), and it was the way He revealed Himself to the patriarchs. This is evident in His words to Moses: "I appeared to Abraham, to Isaac and to Jacob as God Almighty, but by my name the LORD [Yahweh] I did not make myself known to them" (Exod. 6:3, NIV).

> We prefer the quick, prophetic word to personal wrestling with Him in prayer and intercession—and devouring His Word as it is revealed in Scripture.

Similarly, the disclosure of God's name in Exodus 3:14 was almost immediately followed by signs, wonders, and miracles. With the possible exception of the birth of Isaac, supernatural events were largely withheld from the patriarchs until the era of Moses' ministry (his rod turning into a serpent, the plagues on Egypt, the crossing of the Red Sea, and the provision of manna).

Second, God's Word is to be magnified above His name because the Word is an integral part of the plan of salvation. We are saved in precisely the same way Abraham was saved: by believing God's promise—His Word. In fact, Abraham became Paul's chief example of justification by faith.

Abraham's justification occurred long before the signs and wonders that he experienced (the provision of a son and a sacrificial ram). Instead, Abraham was justified when he placed faith in the promises of God (Gen. 15:6). Ultimately, we are not saved by signs and wonders but by believing the Word—the promise. That, in a word, is the gospel.

And yet a third—and deeper—reason for God's exaltation of His Word above His name may be that we might get to know God for who He is in Himself. This takes time. It means devouring His Word—the Scriptures—just in order to know Him. If you want to know God, it is required that you spend time with Him alone in prayer and spend time in His Word—not just to see what will "preach" or "teach" or give you a quick sense of direction.

A recent poll of pastors, church leaders, and clergymen on both sides of the Atlantic revealed that the average church leader spends four minutes a day in quiet time and personal devotions. And we wonder why the church is powerless? Martin Luther wrote in his journal, "I have a very busy day today; must spend not two, but three, hours in prayer." John Wesley was on his knees every day at 4:00 a.m. for two hours. But where are the Wesleys and Luthers?

We are all too busy, so getting to know God for His own sake has less appeal nowadays. We prefer the quick prophetic word to personal wrestling with Him in prayer and intercession—and devouring His Word as it is revealed in Scripture. I recently watched a religious program on television that began something like this: "You will be glad you stayed tuned because we have a word—a *rhema* for you!"

That is what we all seem to want, myself included. *Rhema* is a biblical word—used seventy times in the New Testament—sometimes indicating what is prophetic, personal, and immediate. For this reason, many prefer the prophetic word to the expository word that emerges in preaching and teaching. Sometimes I think that a preoccupation with the *rhema* word rather than the written Word is like going to McDonald's or Burger King: quick, fast food, which makes us flabby but not very healthy.

KNOWING THE AUTHOR

One of my predecessors at Westminster Chapel, Dr. Martyn Lloyd-Jones, has published many books of sermons. He graciously made himself available to me during the first four years I was at Westminster Chapel. There were two ways of learning from him: reading his books and asking him questions.

Most people did not have the latter privilege as I did. But the way I showed the most respect and appreciation for this man was to have read his books first before asking him his view about this or that verse in the Bible. To talk with him was like getting his *rhema* word, but to read his books is what truly enabled me to know him.

God is gracious to us, too. He understands how we want—and sometimes need—a word fitly spoken in a time of stress. "He knows how we are formed, he remembers that we are dust" (Ps. 103:14, NIV). But to those who sit at His feet and learn of Him, the reward is incalculable. In John 14:26, Jesus told the disciples that the Holy Spirit would remind them of what He had taught them. I suspect the disciples often thought, *Will I remember this?*, when they were hearing Him teach or give a parable. The problem is, if we haven't learned anything, there will be nothing in our heads to be reminded of!

If you are empty-headed when you receive the laying on of hands, you will be empty-headed when you get off the floor! It is the promise of the Holy Spirit that should motivate us to receive good teaching, give good teaching, and memorize Scripture verses (an art that has almost perished from the earth). The coming of the Holy Spirit in power makes the discipline of receiving teaching, memorizing Scripture, and wrestling with His Word all worthwhile.

A few years ago, the late John Wimber invited me to have a meal with him in London. The same day I was to meet him the Spirit gave me a word for him. It made me a little nervous. In fact, I did not eat when I sat with him and his wife, Carol, that evening. I waited for the right moment to say, "I have a word for you." He looked at me and said, "Shoot." I did.

"John, when I heard you speak at Royal Albert Hall on Monday evening I agreed with what you said," I began. I then reminded him of his own words: "Luther and Calvin gave us the Word in the sixteenth century, but God wants us to do the works in the twentieth century." He agreed that is what he said. "John," I said with some fear and trembling, "you are teaching pharaohs who knew not Joseph. In other words, people in the twentieth century don't know the Word to begin with."

He dropped his knife and fork, pointed to his chest, and said, "You have just touched in the very vortex of where I am." He went on to say, "I receive your word."

A clear understanding of the gospel should be prior to the prophetic word or signs and wonders. I wish it were not the case, but most people cannot write in a sentence—much less a paragraph—what justification by faith means. Some ministers and church leaders would have the same problem. And, yet, it is also true that the Word alone is not enough.

That is why the Word must be joined by the Spirit. When Paul said that his gospel came not in word only, he implied that it could have been that way. But he was able to say in 1 Thessalonians 1:5 that it came also with power. I fear that too much of my own preaching and teaching have been simply with words. That is not good enough. We need the Spirit to produce the power that not only applies the Word effectually, but also that accompanies the Word with what is unmistakably supernatural. Then—and only then—will we see the world turned upside down.

ISHMAEL OR ISAAC?

One way I have described the relationship of the emphases of the Spirit and the Word is the relationship between Ishmael and Isaac. So obsessed was he with making God's promises come to pass, that Abraham took matters into his own hands and impregnated his servant Hagar. Abraham believed that Ishmael was to be the promised son, but he was wrong.

Then came the wonderful news: Sarah was pregnant. But was this good news for Abraham? He now had to completely adjust to the idea of Ishmael not being the promised son. The thought of Sarah being pregnant was not only laughable but also disrupting.

> The coming of the Holy Spirit in power makes the discipline of receiving teaching, memorizing Scripture, and wrestling with His Word all worthwhile.

It is my view that what we have largely seen in the church up until now is Ishmael. God had a definite plan for Ishmael—and it is my own opinion that we have hardly begun to see what God had in mind. And, yet, Ishmael, though loved by Abraham, was not what God ultimately had in mind. God had Isaac in mind from the beginning but waited a good while before He revealed this.

God declared that His covenant would be established with Isaac—an "everlasting covenant" (Gen. 17:19). Through Isaac, Abraham would be "heir of the world" and a father "of many nations" (Rom. 4:13, 17). Ishmael represents what those on both the Word side and the Spirit side have understood as the ultimate promise of what God wants to do.

Those on the Word side tend to see sound doctrine and faithful expository preaching as being "as good as it gets." Those on the Spirit side tend to see the

155

movement of the Spirit in Pentecostal and Charismatic circles of the last century as being "as good as it gets." I believe that both perspectives are wrong. Isaac is coming. He is being birthed as you read these lines. Moreover, the promise concerning the spontaneous combustion of the Word and the Spirit will be in proportion to the original promise about Isaac—far greater than the one regarding Ishmael.

A REMARRIAGE

For the Word without the Spirit and the Spirit without the Word—though achieving a lot—hardly compare with what is coming when the two are joined once again. It is then that the ministers of God will stand where no one has stood since the days of the early church.

This message probably offends some. It offended Abraham when he first heard it. "Word" people may say, "Are you telling us we don't have a place for the Holy Spirit?" I would answer that most evangelicals have a "soteriological" doctrine of the Spirit (the Spirit applies the Word but does not manifest Himself immediately and directly).

Spirit people may say, "Are you telling us we don't preach the Word?" I would answer that too many Charismatics and Pentecostals stress the *rhema* of the prophetic but often seem utterly bored with the *logos* of expository preaching. I humbly plead with you to consider these lines. Would you not agree that we need more than what we have at the moment?

The world is going to hell, taking almost no notice of the church, and we delude ourselves if we say that what we have is "as good as it gets." There is more. Let us fall to our knees and look to heaven with the Bible in one hand and the other reaching out to all God will give us. And it just may be that He will look down on us with pity and bless us. The result will be that both sound theology and the supernatural be rewed in our time.

ABOUT THE AUTHOR

R. T. Kendall was the pastor of Westminster Chapel in London for twenty-five years. Educated at Southern Baptist Theological Seminary and Oxford University, Kendall is the author of more than thirty books, including the bestseller *Total Forgiveness*. He lives with his wife, Louise, in Key Largo, Florida.

FOR FURTHER STUDY

R. T. Kendall, *The Anointing: Yesterday, Today, Tomorrow*

R. T. Kendall, *Understanding Theology: The Means of Developing a Healthy Church in the Twenty-first Century*

R. T. Kendall, *The Sensitivity of the Spirit*

CHAPTER 23

True or False?

—GARY B. MCGEE

SUMMARY

For too long, we've used our spiritual experience as an excuse for not digging into God's Word more thoroughly. It's time to put our theology to the test of the final authority—Scripture.

I DON'T CARE WHAT you say the Bible means on this point," a student once said to me. "I know from experience that it isn't that way!" Though sincere, this misguided declaration simply demonstrates the ongoing need for believers to recognize how biblical truths surpass the human experience in authority. Scripture alone is "God-breathed and is useful for teaching, rebuking, correcting and training in righteousness, so that the man of God may be...equipped for every good work" (2 Tim. 3:16–17, NIV).

Since biblical times, conflicts over correct teaching have separated believers or even led to their departure from the faith. Satan's temptation to Eve began with "Did God really say...?" In the New Testament, Paul alerted Timothy to teachers of "false doctrines," characterized by "an unhealthy interest in controversies and quarrels about words that result in envy, strife, malicious talk, evil suspicions and constant friction." They had rejected the "sound instruction of our Lord Jesus Christ" and "godly teaching" (1 Tim. 6:3–5, NIV).

CHALLENGES FOR TEACHERS

Controversies over scriptural statements still trouble believers today. The post-modern culture in which Christians find themselves casts doubts on whether any absolute meaning can be attached to a text of the Bible. A verse may suggest one thing to you, while another person may propose an equally valid but different interpretation. From another angle, certain authors in the Pentecostal/Charismatic tradition have employed "revelation knowledge" to interpret Scripture, masking a thinly veiled twisting of verses to fit pet teachings. Ignoring basic rules for interpreting the Bible has sometimes led to personal opinions becoming dogmas for others to follow.

Proper biblical interpretation begins with the recognition that Holy Scripture is the yardstick for faith and practice. This means that the Bible always ranks above expositions of its contents, written and oral teachings that Martin Luther placed in the category of "tradition." Tradition includes creeds, notes in annotated Bibles, commentaries, systematic theologies, popular books on the Christian life, Sunday school quarterlies, and sermons—as well as the pronouncements of contemporary apostles and prophets.

Interestingly, the Greek word for *heresy* (*hairesis*) ranges in meaning from an "opinion" or "school of thought" ("the party [*hairesis*] of the Sadducees" [Acts 5:17, NIV]), to "the distortion of Christian belief and practice." ("They will secretly introduce destructive heresies [*haireseis*], even denying the sovereign Lord who bought them" [2 Pet. 2:1, NIV].)

Heresies vexed early Christianity and prompted the gathering of church councils to resolve them. Troublesome teachings in the Pentecostal/Charismatic tradition have usually emerged from three dynamics: an overly zealous restorationism, the absorption of wrong cultural values, and heretical ideas in the marketplace that contest historic Christian beliefs.

RESTORING NEW TESTAMENT PRACTICES

The Pentecostal movement burst on the scene at the turn of the twentieth century, filled with an unbounded confidence that the "last days" outpouring of the Holy Spirit would restore the power of the New Testament church. Spirit-filled believers could now speedily evangelize the world. Baptism in the Holy Spirit, prayer for the sick, power to cast out demons, and the reappearance of the gifts of the Spirit all came in the package that had been foretold by the prophet Joel (Joel 2:28–29). A few enthusiasts claimed to be divinely commissioned new "apostles."

At the Topeka, Kansas, revival in 1901, Charles Parham and his students believed that God had conferred on them the languages of the world to expedite missionary evangelism, just as they believed it had happened on the day of Pentecost. Five years later in Los Angeles, participants at the Azusa Street revival testified to the same and initially refused to use musical instruments and hymnals in their attempt to emulate the "pure" worship of the early church. But, most importantly, the "apostolic faith" with its baptism and gifts of the Spirit had been restored.

> Despite the establishment of training schools, Pentecostals and independent Charismatics have paid a horrific price for minimizing the value of ministerial education.

Nonetheless, this restorationist upsurge often left the "saints"—as early Pentecostals referred to themselves—wondering if there were more things to be restored. Pentecostal pioneer Howard Goss was recalled by his wife, Ethel, in *The Winds of God: The Story of the Early Pentecostal Movement (1901–1914) in the Life of Howard A. Goss.* In the book, Ethel recalls Howard as saying, "Walking in the light of God's revelation was considered the guarantee of unbroken fellowship with God."[1]

As a result, preachers felt great pressure to "dig up a new slant on some Scripture, or get some new revelation to his heart every so often." Indeed, "one who did not propagate it, defend it, and let it be known that if necessary he was prepared to lay down his life for it" could only be considered "slow, dull, and unspiritual," Goss says.[2] In this zealous atmosphere, anyone courageous enough to start a Bible institute faced a storm of criticism. It was feared that formal education might short-circuit the power of the Holy Spirit by intellectualizing the faith. With the Holy Spirit as the revealer of new truths, who needed a diploma?

Consequently, many evangelists and pastors with little or no education found themselves ill-prepared to lead congregations to maturity and disciple new believers. Despite the establishment of training schools, Pentecostals and independent Charismatics have paid a horrific price for minimizing the value of ministerial education.

Beginning in 1913, a new "restored" teaching, derived from the Jesus-centered piety of early Pentecostalism, divided the faithful. Rejecting the doctrine of the Trinity of God in three persons, advocates replaced it with only one person in the Godhead: Jesus Christ. A valid water baptism, therefore, had to be done in the name of Jesus (Acts 2:38). For many "Jesus Name" or "Oneness" Pentecostals, salvation and Spirit baptism were the same, with the saints expected to be speaking in tongues when they came out of the waters of baptism, despite the lack of any example of this happening in the Book of Acts.

With this teaching—purportedly the last dynamic of New Testament Christianity to be restored—they revived a heresy labeled *modal monarchianism* (God revealed Himself in three "modes": Father, Son, and Holy Spirit), which an ancient church council had condemned.

With the coming of the "New Order of the Latter Rain" revival movement in 1948, proponents pushed for more restorations: the impartation of the gifts of the Holy Spirit through the laying on of hands, the divine bestowal of unlearned human languages for missionary evangelism that early Pentecostals had touted, and the "manifestation of the sons of God"—the "overcomers"—a mighty End-Time army of victorious, faith-filled believers who would overcome sickness and not die in this life.

Later in the century, more new teachings appeared, among them the beliefs that Christians can be possessed by demons, that the spiritual realm has been organized around "territorial demons," which require "binding" (Matt. 18:18) before effective evangelism can commence, and that Christians can and should converse with angels.

Apart from the Oneness doctrine of the Godhead, none of these teachings amount to "heresy" in the traditional sense. Nevertheless, they have all generated elitism and disunity, producing a similar kind of "party" spirit that had wounded the congregation at Corinth. (See 1 Corinthians 1:10–12.)

Every revival movement in the history of Christianity has produced some measure of discord, and each one has claimed to have new insights and has called for reform. But renewal always causes friction with those satisfied with the status quo. The following words of Jesus summon the "renewed" to exhibit humility in relationships: "A new command I give you: Love one another. As I have loved you, so you must love one another. By this all men will know that you are my disciples, if you love one another" (John 13:34–35, NIV).

BOWING TO THE CULTURE

Like other Christians around the world, Pentecostals and Charismatics are products of their respective cultures. In North America, Pentecostals benefited from the social and economic lift after World War II.

The doctrine of divine healing, which had originally promised immediate physical healing through the prayer of faith, became enlarged to include material prosperity. Faith-healing evangelists, who had taught that the atonement of Christ guaranteed spiritual and physical blessing, now claimed that with sufficient faith, believers could get their fair share of the American dream.

The customary greeting found in 3 John 2, "Beloved, I wish above all things that thou mayest prosper and be in health, even as thy soul prospereth" (KJV), became loaded with more guarantees of cash and comforts than John could have imagined.

This new "truth"—luckily discovered within the context of the robust American economy with its seemingly boundless opportunities for financial gain—prompted faith teachers to reexamine such passages as John 16:23 where Jesus says, "I tell you the truth, my Father will give you whatever you ask in my name" (NIV).

Some proposed that the human tongue could function as a "creative force," meaning that whatever a person *confessed*, that person would *possess*. While the encouragement to exercise greater faith for Christian living has undoubtedly borne fruit, the practical application frequently inspired the faithful to *claim* higher salaries, expensive homes, better cars, and, in some cases, to ignore medical attention. Late in life, Kenneth E. Hagin Sr. wisely tried to slam the brakes on the excesses with his book *The Midas Touch*.

> At the beginning of a new century, the Pentecostal/Charismatic community needs skilled teachers who can successfully address the intellectual and spiritual issues of the day, refute harmful teachings, and detect the pitfalls of the prevailing culture.

The eagerness to define God's "blessings" by the consumer values of American culture pushed into the background the "kingdom values" taught by Jesus. (See Matthew 6:19–21.) For some, the path to blessing as defined by God has intersected with the four-lane boulevard of human greed.

It has further distorted the nature of the Christian world mission. Exporting the "health and wealth" gospel has made little sense in cultures plagued by hunger, poverty, and economic and political oppression. Still, this points to a larger issue that prosperous Christians everywhere must face: whether their prophetic witness against materialism and exploitation measures up to that of Jesus.

HERESIES STILL MATTER

The Pentecostal/Charismatic tradition has never been without severe critics. Charges of heresy, false doctrine, and fanaticism circulated widely in the early years. By the middle of the twentieth century, these accusations diminished as Pentecostals joined forces with other evangelical Christians.

Oneness Pentecostals, however, remained sidelined due to their view of the Godhead, though they remained firmly Pentecostal and evangelical in other doctrines. Contrary to the charges of recent "heresy hunters" and "cult watchers," they do not serve a different God or profess something other than salvation as a gift of grace. Ironically, Oneness Pentecostals speak about God as Father, Son, and Holy Spirit as much as their Trinitarian siblings.

This is not to suggest that their views of the Godhead and water baptism stand without need of correction or lack insight. The relationship of the "persons" within the Trinity ultimately remains a mystery that will always press the limitations of human reasoning. Recent discussions on the theological border between Oneness and Trinitarian Pentecostals at the annual meetings of the Society for Pentecostal Studies have been beneficial, breaking down stereotypical views of each other's positions and building bridges of understanding.

Unfortunately, the revival of another ancient heresy imperils the very nature of evangelism. The doctrine of the "reconciliation of all things," a form of universalism asserting that all will eventually be redeemed through Christ, first became prominent through the teachings of the second-century church father Origen. Condemned as heresy by an ancient church council, it has resurfaced at different times. While all have sinned, its proponents say, punishment has a remedial purpose even after death. For those unconverted during their lifetimes, salvation will come after an unspecified period of purification in a form of purgatory. In this way, all of humankind will ultimately be saved.

Notwithstanding the appeal of this scenario, Jesus pronounced that the unrepentant would face "eternal punishment" in contrast to the righteous who would enjoy "eternal life" (Matt. 25:46, NIV). In writing to the Thessalonians about the coming judgment at Jesus' return, Paul warned that "those who do not know God and do not obey the gospel of our Lord Jesus . . . will be punished with everlasting destruction and shut out from the presence of the Lord and from the majesty of his power" (2 Thess. 1:8–9, NIV).

The clarity of these verses trumps any interpretation based on wishful thinking about the fate of the spiritually lost. Biblical Christian mission is rooted in the certainty of the gospel, life after death, the forthcoming judgment of all peoples, and the everlasting duration of heaven and hell. The famous evangelist Dwight L. Moody said it well: "I look upon this world as a wrecked vessel.... God has given me a lifeboat and said to me, 'Moody, save all you can.'"

THE CROWN OF TEACHING

At the beginning of a new century, the Pentecostal/Charismatic community needs skilled teachers who can successfully address the intellectual and spiritual issues of the day, refute harmful teachings, and detect the pitfalls of the prevailing culture.

This form of servanthood to Christ represents a "gift" of the risen Christ to the church. Paul listed teachers, along with apostles, prophets, evangelists, and pastors, as gifts who "prepare God's people for works of service, so that the body of Christ may be built up until we all reach unity in the faith and in the knowledge of the Son of God and become mature, attaining to the whole measure of the fullness of Christ. Then we will no longer be infants, tossed back and forth by the waves, and blown here and there by every wind of teaching" (Eph. 4:12–14, NIV).

Over the course of Christian history, the church has counted among its greatest heroes, teachers and scholars (for example, Augustine, Aquinas, Luther, Calvin, and Wesley) who have enriched believers with their spiritual insights and passed them on to succeeding generations. As gifts to the church—whether ordained in the traditional sense or not—they should excel at "speaking the truth in love" (v. 15, NIV).

After weeks spent discipling converts at Thessalonica, Paul expressed to them the aspiration of Christian teachers past and present: "For what is our hope, our joy, or the crown in which we will glory in the presence of our Lord Jesus when he comes? Is it not you? Indeed, you are our glory and joy" (1 Thess. 2:19–20, NIV).

ABOUT THE AUTHOR

Gary B. McGee, PhD, is professor of church history and Pentecostal studies at the Assemblies of God Theological Seminary in Springfield, Missouri. His latest book is *People of the Spirit: The Assemblies of God.*

FOR FURTHER STUDY

Benny C. Aker and Gary B. McGee, *Signs & Wonders in Ministry Today*

Jack Deere, *Surprised by the Power of the Spirit*

J. Rodman Williams, *Renewal Theology* (3 volumes)

CHAPTER 24

The Character of a Teacher

—JOHN PAUL JACKSON

SUMMARY

Don't underestimate how God prepares His teachers in the secret place. Private victories are foundations for a public ministry.

BOYS, I'M PLEASED to announce that Jimmy Claven is this year's coach for a day."

My heart sank. I couldn't believe my high school baseball coach picked Jimmy Claven to be "coach for a day" when I was having a banner year. I had been waiting for two years to be named "coach for a day." Success in baseball came easily for me. This was my year! Jimmy Claven was a nice kid, but he wasn't the best player on the team. I was having a record-breaking year and couldn't believe that my performance had gone unnoticed. A mistake must have been made. Perhaps it was a joke?

I went to the coach and smiled knowingly. "John Paul," he told me, "you have very good natural talent. Because of your hand-eye coordination, you have a very good batting average. But you don't know the first thing about coaching. If a batter missed a ball, you'd simply tell him to quit taking his eye off the ball.

"On the other hand," he continued, "Jimmy would coach the batter about putting too much weight on his back leg when he swung, or he might notice that the batter was not getting proper arm extension. Jimmy would know if the player was watching the ball as it left the pitcher's hand with his front eye or his back eye." The coach went on to say: "Jimmy knows baseball because he has had to study to improve himself. All you had to do is show up and swing the bat."

Hearing those words from my coach stunned me—but he was right. I had no idea how to teach someone how to improve his or her techniques. What I did came easily for me. That experience changed me. I have since applied it to all aspects of my life, including my spiritual life. As a result, some years ago I embarked on a journey to discover how to teach others what I know and do.

BUILDING CHARACTER

It takes people with godly character and habits to serve effectively in the kingdom of God. While there are many talented and anointed teachers, those who have a foundation of godly character (moral excellence) teach with more than their words; they teach with their lifestyles in ways that are truly transformational. Who we are as teachers is just as important as what we teach. It is who we are, more than what we know, that inspires change in another person's life.

> While there are many talented and anointed teachers, those who have a foundation of godly character (moral excellence) teach with more than their words; they teach with their lifestyles in ways that are truly transformational.

We must decide to take the necessary steps to strengthen our own moral legacies by practicing what we preach. Moral excellence can only be built through Bible study, quiet times with God, and a history of making right choices—what I like to call "hidden victories." These hidden victories ensure long-term success in the kingdom.

Sadly, character is a topic that the church often talks about but rarely teaches people how to walk out. All of us can remember examples of people who were put into positions of leadership based on their anointing and gifts, but they lacked character. We also remember the disheartening results. Such leaders had great charisma and great anointing, but, like Samson, their moral deficiencies brought their demise.

When leaders have talents that are greater in measure than their characters, they experience stress and anxiety, feeling the pressure to perform and succeed. They have a reputation they feel they must maintain. Deep inside they are afraid to let God do the work of advancement and recognition in their ministries and callings. So, they begin to rush ahead of God and promote themselves before they are truly "matured" by God.

As I have studied the Bible and meditated on God's view of character, I have concluded that there are four components that evidence healthy, godly character: love, integrity, maturity, and an abundance mentality.

Love is essential to every ministry. The apostle Paul made this clear when he wrote, "If I speak God's Word with power, revealing all his mysteries and making everything plain as day, and if I have faith that says to a mountain, 'Jump,' and it jumps, but I don't love, I'm nothing" (1 Cor. 13:2, THE MESSAGE).

What a statement! Throughout the history of God's kingdom, there have been "gifted nothings"—people who have done miraculous work but who never truly understood the need for intimacy with God and the love of Christ. No wonder love is the first fruit of the Holy Spirit listed in Galatians 5:22!

Integrity is the act of being entirely honest at all times. Teachers must forge a foundation of trust with those whom they are mentoring, equipping, and leading. If a teacher has integrity, a student will remember what he or she teaches because the student will have seen the teacher's actions match his or her words. Jesus had the highest level of integrity possible; His disciples knew He practiced what He preached. This inspired them to strive to be like Jesus, both in word and deed.

Maturity involves sound reasoning and decision making. When someone has walked through the trials and fires of life, spiritual maturity is developed. God says in Isaiah 48:10, "Behold, I have refined you, but not as silver; I have tested you in the furnace of affliction." This furnace is at full flame when we are off the platform, living our lives away from the public eye.

It takes the private testing of God for a person's character to solidify and mature. The result of maturity is meekness, which is how we interact with others. Maturity allows us to esteem others higher than ourselves. Maturity allows us to see God's plan in our chaos.

An abundance mentality sees God as having so much talent and anointing to give people and recognizes that none of us have a corner on the market. Embracing an abundance mentality requires that we demonstrate humility. It's not about us anyway; it's about God and His kingdom. Anything less allows jealousy to manifest in our lives. We must have a heart that blesses the gifts others have, knowing that all gifts are given by God to equip others and to further advance God's kingdom on earth.

WHO'S WATCHING

We cannot become truly great in God's kingdom unless we walk through adversity, pain, and difficulty. Here are some examples from God's Word:

- Joseph was made second in command of Egypt after years of wrongful imprisonment and unfair slavery.

- Gideon delivered the Israelites from their enemies after struggling with insecurity and fear.

- Samuel left his parents and served in the often lonely temple before growing into a great prophet and judge.

- David became a beloved king after years of living in caves and dodging death threats.

- Paul was blinded and then persecuted as his ministry grew. These private battles forged great leaders for God.

Likewise, hidden victories in the daily grind of life form a foundation for how we operate publicly. What do we do when no one is watching us? How are we treating our spouses? Are we devoting quality time with our children? Are we being generous financially and spiritually? Have we overcome issues of rejection and fear that plague our lives? Have we restored broken relationships? Are we speaking blessings over others?

It takes hundreds of these seemingly insignificant, private victories to form a solid foundation of character upon which God places the weightiness of public ministry.

When David sought Saul's approval before facing Goliath, he told the king about his private victories: "Your servant has killed both lion and bear; and this uncircumcised Philistine will be like one of them, seeing he has defied the armies of the living God" (1 Sam. 17:36, NIV).

David's history of hidden victories as a shepherd gave him the faith and confidence to face Goliath publicly as a protector of Israel's future. A foundation of character, formed humbly and quietly in the hidden moments of life, had been built in the future king's life. Little did David know how these events would allow God to use him one day. As we overcome our personal battles, God can trust us with the great responsibility of teaching others.

I believe we are tripartite human beings, composed of three parts: body, which is flesh, bone, and blood; soul, which is our mind, will, and emotions; and spirit, which is the source of wisdom, communion, and conscience.

All ministry—teaching, mentoring, discipling, and leading others—flows from one of the three parts of our beings. Therefore, teaching others can be classified in three parallel ways, according to which part of our beings the teaching flows: productive teaching, creative teaching, or spiritual teaching.

Productive teaching is sparked when our bodies are in control. It's about doing, accomplishing, and reaching a mandated quantity or volume. For teachers, it's manifested in a rigid adherence to predetermined lesson plans. Left unchecked, it will turn our love of teaching into a job, because the battle against time will consume us.

Productive teaching doesn't bring about long-term change in anyone or anything; it's simply an endless stream of information given to students in order to achieve higher test scores. This level of teaching does not demand understanding or the application of the material to life.

> If a teacher has integrity, a student will remember what he or she teaches, because the student will have seen the teacher's actions match his or her words.

Creative teaching is produced by our souls; it can also be called imaginative teaching. Our human emotions produce a passion to teach, while our wills decide to capture those feelings in the lesson. Our minds then fuse this passion and desire into a complete effort.

Teachers who instruct and coach from this perspective feel as though they have to devise something and formulate ideas. Creative teaching can change a person for the short term, but it has no eternal effect on its students. It sounds intelligent, but it isn't breathed upon by God. Thus, students may apply the learned material to their current tasks, but they do not understand how to apply it to their lives.

Spiritual teaching flows from communion with the Holy Spirit. It involves communication from the teacher's spirit to the student's spirit through the power of the Holy Spirit. The human spirit is what connects each of us to God.

Because of the work of redemption, our spirits are intermingled, and the Spirit of God within us is imparted to students. The Spirit uses the soul and body to accomplish God's planned, incredible work.

While there are many gifted teachers, I believe that only a Christian can teach spiritually. When the Holy Spirit communicates through us to others it is transformational. The Holy Spirit's work results in an eternal change in a person's life. "I will not be the same," the student says. "This has changed my life." While "soulish" or creative teaching can cause temporary change in a person, spiritual teaching changes a man or woman for eternity.

The challenge for teachers, therefore, is to listen carefully to the heartbeat of the Holy Spirit. We must continually be sensitive to listening to the Holy Spirit and to cleaning out the issues that keep our souls in the drivers' seats of our lives. We must develop a history of hidden victories.

It takes discipline and practice to fully understand the distinction between what is our own soul and what is the leading of the Holy Spirit. We must be committed to allowing more and more of His essence to flow through us.

God wants to teach us today what will inspire others tomorrow. He has a vantage point of what will be, not just what is or has been. We as teachers have been content to grasp at slivers of spiritual insights, but the Holy Spirit wants to give us fuller concepts of God and His ways.

Teaching is a weighty responsibility, given by God to those whom He can trust to carry it. As teachers, we must develop godly character and walk in greater integrity and maturity so that we can understand God's plans and visions for those whom we have been entrusted to teach.

Only the Lord, by helping us practice our private victories, can make our lives a lasting—and public—contribution to His eternal kingdom. Only then can we help others reach the exciting destinies for which God created them.

ABOUT THE AUTHOR

John Paul Jackson is the founder of Streams Ministries an in-depth, prophetic, teaching ministry (www.streamsministries.com). He travels around the world teaching on hearing God, dreams, visions, and the realm of the supernatural.

FOR FURTHER STUDY

John Paul Jackson, *Needless Casualties of War*

John Paul Jackson, *I AM: Inheriting the Fullness of God's Names*

John Paul Jackson, *Breaking Free of Rejection*

CHAPTER 25

A Teacher and a Mother
—MATTHEW GREEN

SUMMARY

A tribute to the life and ministry of Fuchsia Pickett. Her fifty-plus years of teaching will not be forgotten.

FUCHSIA PICKETT NEVER fit the mold of a Charismatic teacher. Reared in a Methodist family, led to Christ by a Presbyterian friend, educated at John Wesley College, and dramatically healed and filled with the Holy Spirit in a Pentecostal church, Pickett became an icon of unconventional wisdom during her fifty-plus years of ministry.

She stepped into the pulpit at a time when women's callings were typically confined to the nursery, and she taught on the importance of a crucified life when self-promotion and prosperity were the hallmarks of many prominent ministries.

Who knew that one day this unassuming woman would impact some of the church's most influential leaders, including Myles Munroe, Judson Cornwall, Benny Hinn, and others.

On January 30, 2004, at the age of eighty-five, Pickett died peacefully in her Tennessee home and went to be with her beloved Jesus. But her life and her teachings will not soon be forgotten.

EARLY PREPARATION

Pickett was born to God-fearing parents in Axton, Virginia, and faithfully attended a Methodist church during her early years. She married at sixteen, after graduating from high school.

Soon after, Pickett began observing the vibrant faith of a Presbyterian girl with whom she worked. Convicted, Pickett would often lie awake at night questioning whether she would go to heaven.

After attending an evangelistic rally, Pickett fell to her knees in her bedroom and cried out to God. That night, Pickett walked from darkness into light. Soon after, God began speaking to her.

Lying in bed one night, she heard a distinct voice calling her name, and she sensed that the room was filled with the presence of God. "I want you to preach and teach My Word," the voice said.

"I knew I had heard the voice of God," Pickett told *Ministries Today* in her final interview. God opened the door for her to attend John Wesley College in Greensboro, North Carolina, and, later, Martinsville Bible College, Aldergate University, and the University of North Carolina.

THE TEACHER MOVES IN

For the next seventeen years, Pickett traveled throughout the country, preaching and teaching—although it was rare at the time for a woman to do so.

When her father was dying of Hodgkin's disease, Pickett began to notice in her own body symptoms of a debilitating bone disease. "I felt instinctively that my days of ministry would soon be over," she said. Pickett tried to hide her condition from her family until the symptoms became unavoidable, and she found herself in a hospital bed, supported with braces and packed in sandbags to sustain her body.

She had written her own funeral, selected pallbearers, and purchased a tombstone when a friend offered to take her to a meeting at a Pentecostal church. During the service, Pickett heard the Holy Spirit tell her to go forward for prayer. Her weakened body in braces, she dragged herself to the front and spoke to the preacher: "I don't know why I'm here. But I have a feeling that God would like these people to pray for me."

After a simple prayer and a smear of anointing oil, Pickett began limping back to her seat. It was when she reached the seventh pew that she saw her first vision. A voice said to her, "If ye be willing and obedient, ye shall eat the good of the land" (Isa. 1:19, KJV). The voice continued, "Are you willing to be identified with these people—to be one of them?"

"Yes, Lord," she replied and began to lower herself into her seat.

At that moment, Pickett recalled that the power of God struck the base of her neck and coursed through her body. Minutes later, she was dancing and shouting, her unneeded braces clattering to the floor.

An hour later, having exhausted her vocabulary for praising God, Pickett found herself speaking in a language she had never learned or heard before. "Not only was I healed from the top of my head to the tip of my toes," Pickett said, "but I was filled with the Holy Ghost."

"My Teacher moved in," she said. "For the first time in my life I began to understand, through revelation, the same Scriptures I had studied and taught faithfully for many years. They came alive to me, not as information, but as power that was working in me and transforming my life."

DREAMS AND VISIONS

Soon after, God began to reveal Himself to Pickett in dramatic ways. "You run your classes based on sixty-to-ninety-minute sessions," she recalled the Holy Spirit telling her. "I don't. I live here in your spirit. I have moved in to be your Teacher, and My classroom is never closed. I wrote the Book."

Pickett added: "As the Holy Spirit would quicken truth to me, whole books of the Bible would open and relate to each other in my mind. I saw how Leviticus related to Hebrews, Joshua to Ephesians, and I walked the floor, shaking my head and staggering in my ability to grasp it all."

> My Teacher moved in. For the first time in my life I began to understand, through revelation, the same Scriptures I had studied and taught faithfully for many years.

Local Pentecostal pastors caught wind that a Methodist minister had received the Holy Spirit, and soon, Pickett was invited to speak at Pentecostal camp meetings and revival services. As she explained, a Spirit-filled Methodist was a novelty at the time, and her story was welcomed with applause and amazement.

But she was called to do more than just testify. Daily God was revealing truths to her about Himself and His Word. Soon, her Pentecostal friend Ralph Byrd began to notice. "You remind me of a Guernsey cow," he told her one day.

"You are so full of the milk of the Word that you are bursting with it and looking for every calf around you that you can feed."

A TEACHER AND A MOTHER

From that point on, Pickett traveled extensively, preaching at conferences, writing, and teaching at Fountaingate Ministries and Bible College, which she founded in Dallas. Over the years, Pickett became respected as both a teacher and a spiritual mother in the Charismatic movement. Her teaching was a unique marriage of prophetic revelation and verse-by-verse exposition.

Pickett applied theological principles from her formal training, but she never held them too tightly when she felt the Spirit move her in a new direction. "I don't despise what I have studied," Pickett said. "That knowledge of the Word brought me to the point that I could receive true revelation of it."

Unafraid to confront traditional understandings of difficult passages, she often embraced an unconventional allegorical interpretation of Scripture. Pickett described this as the living Word giving her insight into the meaning of the written Word.

For instance, in a vision, Pickett was transported to the court of Esther, where the Spirit explained to her the meaning of the book and its characters: Esther represents the church, Haman the flesh, and Mordecai the Holy Spirit.

While some would argue that books such as Esther and Ruth are historical narratives to be taken in a strictly literal sense, Pickett taught that they are both historical and allegorical—or revelatory. "As Paul said, all these things were examples," she explained. "The Holy Spirit wrote the facts, but He also gave us deeper allegorical truths all the way through."

The core of her teaching, however, was the deeper life, death to self, and the Spirit's empowerment for godly living. "It is obedience to the revelation we receive that enables the Holy Spirit to keep giving us new revelation," she said. "The test of true revelation is the power it has to transform our thinking and our lives to the image of Christ."

Was she afraid of making mistakes? "Not mistakes, but incomplete truths," she said. "No one person has it all because the truth is broken into bits." Never one to hold too tightly to her interpretations, Pickett encouraged her hearers to examine her teachings through the lens of the written Word.

But doctrine was not as much a concern for Pickett as was the disunity and spiritual apathy she saw in the church. Four years after being filled with the Spirit, she received the most dramatic vision of her life, and, like the prophetess Anna, she longed for its fulfillment.

While she was spending the night in a church in Klamath Falls, Oregon, Pickett saw a hydroelectric power plant being built by crews of laborers. It was surrounded by gates and connected to dammed-up rivers, representing streams of church tradition.

Pickett said that there will be a last-days awakening in which God's river of truth will again plow through the mechanisms of the derelict power plant, releasing revival in the nation and around the world.

It's been nearly forty years since Pickett saw the vision, but she held to its reality. "We are coming to the last season," she said. "God is digging out the reservoirs, filling them with His Word, connecting people who are hungry."

THE STATE OF TEACHING

As she looked at the current church culture, Pickett was both encouraged and concerned. "There seems to be a hunger for what God said rather than what so-and-so said," she said. "This hunger will bring in the presence of God. But if you're not hungry, you won't eat."

In order for true renewal to come, Pickett contended that the church has to be cleansed of denominationalism, culture, and prejudice. "We're fighting over a lot of doctrinal nonessentials—man's opinions, like how to have church," she said. "Denominational lines can come down, and we can focus on what we agree on for the sake of relationship."

> I don't despise what I have studied. That knowledge of the Word brought me to the point that I could receive true revelation of it.

Pickett cautioned against minimizing the importance of the Teacher—the Holy Spirit, that is. "He is the unveiler of the teaching," she said. "If we walk with Him, He'll talk to us and lead us beyond just what we're hearing or reading. The Holy Spirit is the Teacher, but the gift of God given to the church is the teaching."

In her last days, Pickett was still exploring challenging books of the Bible—but not the ones most consider difficult. "Ephesians," she says. "It's one of the books of hunger. In other words, it gives insight and provokes hunger, a book to the mature."

She also hinted that she would soon leave this world. In fall 2003, she told a congregation in Lavergne, Tennessee, that she "wouldn't be coming back."

Sue Curran, who pastors Shekinah Church, the Blountville, Tennessee, congregation attended by Pickett since 1988, visited the teacher shortly before her death. "During my last conversation with her, she was desirous to live as long as the Lord wanted her to," Curran says. "Our church prayed to that end."

A LEGACY

As she grew older, Pickett had lost the physical strength of her younger years but none of the passion and good humor. An interviewer once asked her how old she was. "Age is a number, honey," she replied with a smile. "Mine is unlisted."

Although failing health prevented her from maintaining her rigorous speaking schedule, Pickett continued to address the Scriptures with this childlike faith and a sense of mystery, sharing her wisdom with Christian leaders who came to her for insight.

It was always hard to get Pickett to talk about herself, but you never had to look very hard to find someone who was willing to sing her praises. One of her closest earthly friends was Charismatic Bible teacher Judson Cornwall, who had known her since 1961 when she came to his church in Eugene, Oregon.

"Her insight into the Scriptures was phenomenal," said Cornwall recently. "The life that was in her seemed to be available to all who would listen with spiritual ears."

Cornwall attributed Pickett's gifting to an intimate relationship with God. "You had the sense that she heard from the Holy Spirit in her prayer closet, and I happen to know that she had," he said.

Still, Pickett always realized who really deserved the praise. "It's all about knowing who I am in contrast to who He is. It takes your pride down a number of notches," she said. "The praise that I receive doesn't belong to me. I just pass it on to Him—thank Him for it. I'm only the keeper and steward of knowledge—a trusted servant to handle the truth."

ABOUT THE AUTHOR

Matthew D. Green served for four years as editor of *Ministry Today* magazine. He is currently a freelance writer and director of communications for Pioneers, a mission agency supporting more than one hundred eighty church-planting teams among unreached people groups in eighty-two countries. His Web site may be found at www.matthewdgreen.com.

FOR FURTHER STUDY

Fuchsia Pickett, *Stones of Remembrance*

Fuchsia Pickett, *Receiving Divine Revelation*

Fuchsia Pickett, *How to Search the Scriptures*

CHAPTER 26

Stuck on Titles?

— J. LEE GRADY

SUMMARY

Discover the character and calling that must be present in the fivefold offices—regardless of whether or not titles are used.

BACK IN 2001 I had the opportunity to spend eight remarkable days with leaders of China's underground house-church movement. These amazing men and women—all of whom had spent plenty of time in prison for illegally preaching the gospel—were leading massive church networks.

One man known as Brother Z was responsible for a movement of thirteen million Christians! This guy was like an apostle Paul. He had seen miracles, and he also had been beaten and jailed for his faith. I knew he functioned in an apostolic role because he plants churches, trains pastors, coordinates ambitious evangelism projects, and works hard to stop the spread of heresy—which is common in China because of a lack of Bibles. But Brother Z didn't act like a big shot. In fact, when we gathered for meetings he sat near the back of the room.

I felt unworthy to be in this man's presence, but he was always gracious enough to invite me to sit with him at mealtimes. So one evening over a dinner of fish and rice, I asked Brother Z what titles he uses when referring to himself or other leaders. "Do you call yourself an apostle, a bishop, or what?" I asked.

Brother Z smiled innocently. Perhaps my question amused him. "We don't really use titles," he said. "We just prefer to call each other 'brother' or 'sister.'"

His words haunted me during my journey home. When I got back to the United States I found myself wincing when I saw an advertisement for a conference. Under each featured speaker's photograph was his name and title. Apostle this. Prophet that. Bishop whatever. I felt grieved—not because these men and women didn't have the biblical right to use these titles, but because of the way we seem to flaunt them.

In China, apostles are called brothers. They start churches with new converts. Communist police chase them and sometimes torture them. They certainly aren't doing ministry for money. They have no scent of smugness or arrogance. Meanwhile, on this side of the planet, we wear our titles right out in front, flashing in neon on our double-breasted suits. Some pastors today even appoint themselves bishops or apostles, then recruit churches to be "under" them as if they are building an Amway business.

> In some quarters of American Christianity where style is more important than substance, Bishop Big Head and Elder Ego compete with each other for the largest honorariums, the most luxurious accommodations, the biggest entourages, and the grandest entrances.

In some quarters of American Christianity where style is more important than substance, Bishop Big Head and Elder Ego compete with each other for the largest honorariums, the most luxurious accommodations, the biggest entourages, and the grandest entrances. If Jesus rode past them on His donkey, I wonder if they would recognize Him? Would you?

WE NEED LEGITIMATE FIVEFOLD MINISTRY GIFTS TODAY

I've never understood how Charismatics and Pentecostals who believe the gifts of the Holy Spirit remained in operation after the early church age would adopt a cessationist view of the ministry of apostles and prophets. Why would we not need these ministries today, when there is still so much ground to claim for Christ's kingdom?

The question on the table should not be, "Are there apostles today?" That's a dumb question, since the Bible never says the ministry of apostles would vanish before Christ's return, and there are so many gifted people functioning in this vital role today. I've met apostles from Canada, China, Nigeria, Brazil, Argentina, Holland, Ghana, India, Ethiopia, and many other countries. Most Americans have probably never heard of these behind-the-scenes warriors. Our churches today are led predominantly by pastors, but we can't go forward to claim new territory if we don't recognize the need for genuine apostles.

THE TITLE ITSELF ISN'T THE ISSUE

I don't think it's wrong for a man or woman to use a biblical title if that person is called to that office and other leaders have confirmed his or her ministry calling. After all, Paul called himself an *apostle* (although he often called himself "a bondslave of the Lord" instead), and he commissioned Timothy and others to function in fivefold ministry gifts. The calling of God is holy, and it is not to be disparaged. But let's not cheapen it, either.

Perhaps one reason there is so much resistance to the concept of modern apostles is that we have seen too many false apostles—people who claim the office but don't bear the necessary fruit. Surely by now we all know that just because a man has the label on his business card does not make his title legitimate. We must learn to discern between the prophet and the profiteer. Unless counterfeit ministers are taken out of circulation, they devalue everybody else's credibility.

But we can't reject the fivefold ministry just because of the abuses of the past or because the renegades and charlatans are spoiling it for the rest of us. What we must do is demand integrity and require accountability so that only those who are legitimately commissioned by God get the platform they deserve.

JESUS REQUIRES HUMILITY ABOVE ALL

When Jesus knew He only had one last night to teach His disciples, what did He do? He certainly didn't lecture them about the importance of titles. Nor did He hand out name tags. He dressed like a slave, washed His followers' feet, and modeled humility as the most important leadership value.

Since my trip to China—and during subsequent visits with persecuted Christians in Nigeria—I've realized that God is attracted to humility, while He is repulsed by pride. I wonder if the humility I observed in the leaders of China's underground church has anything to do with the fact that they are leading an estimated twenty-five thousand people to Jesus every day? If we want Chinese results, maybe we should adopt their attitudes.

ABOUT THE AUTHOR

J. Lee Grady is the editor of *Charisma* magazine and the author of *10 Lies the Church Tells Women* and *25 Tough Questions About Women and the Church.*

FOR FURTHER STUDY

Bill Hamon, *Apostles, Prophets and the Coming Moves of God: God's End-Time Plans for His Church and Planet Earth*

C. Peter Wagner, *Apostles and Prophets: The Foundation of the Church*

Hector Torres, *The Restoration of the Apostles & Prophets and How it Will Revolutionize Ministry in the 21st Century*

CHAPTER 27

Understanding Your Gifts

EPHESIANS 4:7–13 TELLS us that when Christ ascended to heaven, He widely distributed the fivefold gifts in His body for its edification. As I hope the preceding chapters explain, although many serve in leadership vocationally, the gifts have not been distributed exclusively among those who have been educated as teachers, appointed as bishops, ordained as pastors, sent out as missionaries, and so on.

Whether you are a layperson or clergy, God calls those who are willing and who possess the character and humility He looks for in His servants. Perhaps the discussions in the previous chapters have awakened a desire in you to serve on a deeper level in His kingdom. Perhaps you seek to better understand your own calling.

The following is a list of questions that will help you as a reader begin the journey to finding out where you fit in the harvest field. It is not intended as an exhaustive list, but as you find yourself answering yes to questions in each category, it may be an indicator of God's gifting in your life.

Remember: the fivefold ministry gifts are ultimately not titles but activities.

For instance, an evangelist is not an evangelist unless he or she preaches the gospel and wins souls for the kingdom. Ultimately, your gift will be authenticated, not by the title that you are assigned, but by the evidence of God's anointing on your life as He empowers you to build up His people and bring His message to those who are lost.

APOSTLE

- I long to take the gospel and establish the church in unreached areas.

- I possess a gift for recruiting, networking, and mobilizing leaders for evangelism, discipleship, and community transformation.

- I seek to be innovative and creative in my approach to bringing the gospel to unreached people.

- I possess the humility and balance in leadership that causes others to look to me for guidance and spiritual mentoring.

- I sometimes feel dissatisfied with what I perceive as institutionalism and rigidness in church organizational structures.

PROPHET

- I possess a concern for justice and righteousness, which often prompts me to speak on behalf of God and the expectations of His Word.

- I engage in intercessory prayer in which I sense strategic plans for spiritual warfare of which I would not be aware through human understanding.

- I possess an uncanny boldness and sensitivity for communicating corrective messages to God's people, both corporately and personally.

- I am zealous when I feel God's name is misrepresented by the church or other Christians.

- I often experience spiritual direction and promptings with information of which I would not humanly be aware.

Evangelist

- I find myself exploring unique strategies for sharing the gospel with unbelievers.

- I possess a burning passion to see souls brought into the kingdom.

- I experience ongoing grief and sadness when considering the plight of the lost.

- I am known by other Christians for my boldness in communicating the gospel.

- I find myself dissatisfied and irritated when I'm in a church setting where I know sinners are present and the gospel is ineffectively or inadequately presented.

Pastor

- I am often sought out by those seeking advice, prayer, and spiritual direction.

- I feel concern for the nurture and shepherding of my fellow believers.

- I work to protect fellow believers from false teaching and destructive leadership patterns.

- I am considered patient and longsuffering with the faults and inadequacies of others.

- I take responsibility for the spiritual maturity and growth of my fellow believers.

Teacher

- I am systematic in my approach to studying and communicating concepts and seek to discover truths of application in biblical principles.

- I am passionate in studying Scripture and enjoy research and the communication of information and principles that I discover.

- I am able to distill complex concepts into easily understood ideas that resonate with my hearers.

- I find myself dissatisfied and irritated when I encounter what I perceive as shallow or heretical preaching or teaching.

- I long to apply the results of my academic studies in my own life so that my teaching may be authentic in word *and* deed.

Notes

CHAPTER 4
THE DOC RESPONDS

1. David Barrett, *World Christian Encyclopedia* (Oxford, UK: Oxford University Press, 2001).

CHAPTER 8
PUTTING PERSONAL PROPHECY TO THE TEST

1. Gordon D. Fee, *The First Epistle to the Corinthians* (Grand Rapids, MI: Wm. B. Eerdmans Pub. Co., 1987).

CHAPTER 10
FINDING YOUR PROPHETIC VOICE

1. J. Rodman Williams, *The Era of the Spirit* (South Plainfield, NJ: Logos Publishing, 1971).
2. Bill Hamon, *Prophets and Personal Prophecy* (Shippensburg, PA: Destiny Image Publishers, 1987).
3. Wayne Grudem, *The Gift of Prophecy in the New Testament Church and Today* (Wheaton, IL: Crossway Books, 2000).
4. David Watson, *I Believe in the Church* (Grand Rapids, MI: Wm. B. Eerdmans Pub. Co., 1979).
5. Ernest B. Gentile, *Your Sons & Daughters Shall Prophesy* (Grand Rapids, MI: Chosen Books, 1999).
6. Jack Hayford, *The Beauty of Spiritual Language* (Nashville, TN: Nelson, 1996).
7. Ibid.
8. Cecil Robeck Jr., "The Gift of Prophecy and the All-Sufficiency of Scripture," *Paraclete*, Winter 1979.

CHAPTER 12
MISSION: POSSIBLE

1. Timothy Yates, *The Expansion of Christianity* (Westmont, IL: InterVarsity Press, 2004).
2. Patrick Johnstone and Jason Mandryk, *Operation World* (Waynesboro, GA: Gabriel Resources, n.d.).
3. Samuel Escobar, *The New Global Mission* (Westmont, IL: InterVarsity Press, 2003).
4. Grant McClung, interview with author, April/May 2004.

5. David Shibley, interview with author, April/May 2004.
6. Howard Foltz, interview with author, April/May 2004.
7. Shibley, interview with author, April/May 2004.
8. McClung, interview with author, April/May 2004.
9. Shibley, interview with author, April/May 2004.
10. Foltz, interview with author, April/May 2004.
11. Shibley, interview with author, April/May 2004.
12. Ibid.
13. Foltz, interview with author, April/May 2004.
14. Scott Hinkle, interview with author, April/May 2004.
15. James Davis, interview with author, April/May 2004.
16. Hinkle, interview with author, April/May 2004.
17. Davis, interview with author, April/May 2004.
18. Ibid.
19. Hinkle, interview with author, April/May 2004.
20. Davis, interview with author, April/May 2004.
21. U.S. Center for World Mission, www.uscwm.org.
22. The Barna Update, "Evangelicals Are the Most Generous Givers, But Fewer Than 10% of Born Again Christians Give 10% to Their Church," April 5, 2005, http://www.barna.org/FlexPage.aspx?Page=BarnaUpdate&BarnaUpdateID= 52 (accessed March 21, 2005).
23. U.S. Center for World Mission, www.uscwm.org.
24. Johnstone and Mandryk, *Operation World*.
25. Ibid.
26. Ibid.
27. Foltz, interview with author, April/May 2004.

CHAPTER 14
HOW TO SHARE YOUR FAITH...
WITHOUT LOSING YOUR MIND

1. Bill Bright, *The Coming Revival* (Nashville, TN: New Life Publications, 1995).

CHAPTER 15
THE WORLD IS WAITING

1. Isaac Watts, "When I Survey the Wondrous Cross," Public Domain.

CHAPTER 17
CELL MULTIPLICATION

1. Rebecca Manley Pippert, *Out of the Saltshaker and Into the World* (Westmont, IL: InterVarsity Press, 1999).

2. Rick Richardson, *Evangelism Outside the Box* (Westmont, IL: InterVarsity Press, 2000).
3. Robert Putnam, *Bowling Alone: The Collapse and Revival of American Community* (New York: Simon & Schuster, 2001).

CHAPTER 23
TRUE OR FALSE?

1. Howard A. Goss, *The Winds of God: The Story of the Early Pentecostal Movement (1901–1914) in the Life of Howard A. Goss* (N.p.: Comet Press Books, 1958).
2. Ibid.

Bibliography

Aker, Benny C. and Gary B. McGee. *Signs & Wonders in Ministry Today*. Springfield, MO: Gospel Publishing House, 1996.

Barnett, Tommy. *Adventure Yourself*. Lake Mary, FL: Charisma House, 1999.

———. *Dream Again*. Lake Mary, FL: Charisma House, 1998.

———. *Hidden Power*. Lake Mary, FL: Charisma House, 2002.

———. *Multiplication: Unlock the Biblical Factors to Multiply Your Effectivenes in Leadership & Ministry*. Lake Mary, FL: Charisma House, 1997.

———. *Reaching Your Dreams: 7 Steps for Turning Dreams Into Reality*. Lake Mary, FL: Charisma House, 2005.

———. *There's a Miracle in Your House*. Lake Mary, FL: Charisma House, 1993.

Barrett, David. *World Christian Encyclopedia*. Oxford, UK: Oxford University Press, 2001.

Beacham, Doug. *Plugged In to God's Power*. Lake Mary, FL: Charisma House, 2002.

———. *Rediscovering the Role of Apostles and Prophets*. Franklin Springs, GA: LifeSprings Resources, Inc., n.d.

Bickle, Mike. *Growing in the Prophetic*. Lake Mary, FL: Creation House, 1996.

Bloomer, George. *Authority Abusers: Breaking Free From Spiritual Abuse*. Springdale, PA: Whitaker House, 2002.

Blue, Ken. *Healing Spiritual Abuse: How to Break Free From Bad Church Experiences*. Westmont, IL: InterVarsity Press, 1993.

Bonnke, Reinhard. *Evangelism by Fire: Igniting Your Passion for the Lost*. Orlando, FL: Full Flame, 2002.

———. *Even Greater*. Orlando, FL: Full Flame, 2005.

———. *Mighty Manifestations: The Gifts and Power of the Holy Spirit*. Orlando, FL: Full Flame, 2002.

Boren, M. Scott. *Making Cell Groups Work*. Houston, TX: Cell Group Resources, 2002.

Bright, Bill. *The Coming Revival*. Nashville, TN: New Life Publications, 1995.

Burks, Ron and Vicki Burks. *Damaged Disciples: Casualties of Authoritarian Churches and the Shepherding Movement*. Grand Rapids, MI: Zondervan, 1992.

Cartledge, David. *The Apostolic Revolution*. Orleans, MA: Paraclete Press, n.d.

Cho, David Yonggi. *Successful Home Cell Groups*. Gainesville, FL: Bridge-Logos Publishers, 1981.

Comfort, Ray and Kirk Cameron. *The Way of the Master: How to Share Your Faith Simply, Effectively, Biblically—the Way Jesus Did*. Grand Rapids, MI: Tyndale, 2004.

Comfort, Ray. *Hell's Best Kept Secret*. Springdale, PA: Whitaker House, 1989.

———. *What Did Jesus Do?* N.p.: Genesis Publications, 2005.

———. *What Hollywood Believes: An Intimate Look at the Faith of the Famous*. N.p.: Genesis Publications, 2004.

Comiskey, Joel. *How to Lead a Great Cell Group Meeting…So People Want to Come Back*. Houston TX: Touch Publications, 2001.

Cooke, Graham. *Developing Your Prophetic Gifting*. Grand Rapids, MI: Chosen Books, 2003.

Davis, James O. *The Pastor's Best Friend: The New Testament Evangelist*. Springfield, MO: Gospel Publishing House, 1997.

Dayton, Donald W. *Theological Roots of Pentecostalism*. Peabody, MA: Hendrickson, 1991.

Deere, Jack. *Surprised by the Power of the Spirit*. Grand Rapids, MI: Zondervan, 1996.

———. *The Beginner's Guide to the Gift of Prophecy*. Ann Arbor, MI: Vine Books, 2001.

Dimazio, Frank. *Developing the Prophetic Gifting*. Portland, OR: City Christian Publishing, n.d.

Dobbins, Richard D. *Invisible Imprint: What Others Feel When in Your Presence*. N.p.: VMI, 2002.

———. *Your Spiritual and Emotional Power*. Grand Rapids, MI: Fleming H. Revell Company, 1984.

Dupont, Marc. *Toxic Churches: Restoration from Spiritual Abuse.* Grand Rapids, MI: Chosen, 2004.

Escobar, Samuel. *The New Global Mission.* Westmont, IL: InterVarsity Press, 2003.

Fehlauer, Mike. *Exposing Spiritual Abuse: How to Rediscover God's Love When the Church Has Let You Down.* Lake Mary, FL: Charisma House, 2001.

Foltz, Howard and Ruth Ford. *For Such a Time As This: Strategic Missions Power Shifts for the 21st Century.* N.p.: William Carey Library Publishers, 2001.

Frangipane, Francis. *Discerning of Spirits.* Cedar Rapids, IA: Arrow Publications, 2001.

Gentile, Ernest B. *The Glorious Disturbance.* Grand Rapids, MI: Chosen Books, 2004.

———. *Your Sons & Daughters Shall Prophesy.* Grand Rapids, MI: Chosen Books, 1999.

———. *Prophetic Presbytery in the Local Church.* Portland, OR: City Bible Publishing, 1978.

Goss, Howard A. *The Winds of God: The Story of the Early Pentecostal Movement (1901–1914) in the Life of Howard A. Goss.* N.p.: Comet Press Books, 1958.

Grady, J. Lee. *10 Lies the Church Tells Women.* Lake Mary, FL: Charisma House, 2000.

———. *25 Tough Questions About Women and the Church.* Lake Mary, FL: Charisma House, 2003.

Grudem, Wayne. *The Gift of Prophecy in the New Testament Church and Today.* Wheaton, IL: Crossway Books, 2000.

Hagin Sr., Kenneth E. *The Midas Touch.* Tulsa, OK: Faith Library Publications, 1999.

Hamon, Bill. *Apostles, Prophets and the Coming Moves of God.* Tulsa, OK: Destiny Image, 1997.

———. *Prophets and Personal Prophecy.* Tulsa, OK: Destiny Image, 1987.

———. *Prophets and the Prophetic Movement.* Tulsa, OK: Destiny Image, 1990.

Hayford, Jack. *The Beauty of Spiritual Language.* Nashville, TN: Nelson, 1996.

Hyatt, Eddie L. *2000 Years of Charismatic Christianity*. Lake Mary, FL: Charisma House, 2002.

Jackson, John Paul. *Breaking Free of Rejection*. North Sutton, NH: Streams Ministries, 2004.

———. *I AM: Inheriting the Fullness of God's Names*. North Sutton, NH: Streams Publications, 2003.

———. *Needless Casualties of War*. North Sutton, NH: Streams Publications, 1999.

Jacobs, Cindy. *The Voice of God*. Ventura, CA: Regal Books, 1995.

Johnstone, Patrick and Jason Mandryk. *Operation World*. Waynesboro, GA: Gabriel Resources, n.d.

Kendall, R. T. *In Pursuit of His Glory: My 25 Years at Westminster Chapel*. Lake Mary, FL: Charisma House, 2004.

———. *The Anointing: Yesterday, Today, Tomorrow*. Lake Mary, FL: Charisma House, 2003.

———. *The Sensitivity of the Spirit*. Lake Mary, FL: Charisma House, 2002.

———. *Total Forgiveness*. Lake Mary, FL: Charisma House, 2002.

———. *Understanding Theology: The Means of Developing a Healthy Church in the Twenty-first Century*. Belleville, MI: Christian Focus, 1998.

McClung, Grant L. *Azusa Street and Beyond: Pentecostal Missions and Church Growth in the Twentieth Century*. N.p.: Bridge Publications, 1986.

———. *Globalbeliever.com: Connecting to God's Work in Your World*. Cleveland, TN: Pathway Press, 2000.

McGee, Gary B. *People of the Spirit: The Assemblies of God*. Springfield, MO: Gospel Publishing House, 2004.

Moore, S. David. *The Shepherding Movement: Controversy and Charismatic Ecclesiology*. London, UK: The Continuum International Publishing Group, 2003.

Neighbour, Randall G. *Community Life 101*. Houston, TX: Cell Group Resources, 2004.

Pickett, Fuchsia. *How to Search the Scriptures*. Lake Mary, FL: Charisma House, 1999.

———. *Receiving Divine Revelation*. Lake Mary, FL: Charisma House, 1997.

———. *Stones of Remembrance*. Lake Mary, FL: Charisma House, 1998.

Pippert, Rebecca Manley. *Out of the Saltshaker and Into the World*. Westmont, IL: InterVarsity Press, 1999.

Richardson, Rick. *Evangelism Outside the Box*. Westmont, IL: InterVarsity Press, 2000.

Shibley, David. *The Missions Addiction*. Lake Mary, FL: Charisma House, 2001.

Synan, Vinson. *Century of the Holy Spirit*. Nashville, TN: Nelson, 2001.

———. *The Holiness-Pentecostal Tradition: Charismatic Movements in the Twentieth Century*. Grand Rapids, MI: Wm. B. Eerdmans, 1997.

Torres, Hector. *The Restoration of the Apostles & Prophets and How it Will Revolutionize Ministry in the 21st Century*. Nashville, TN: Nelson, 2001.

Wagner, C. Peter, editor. *Pastors & Prophets: Protocol for Healthy Churches*. Colorado Springs, CO: Wagner Publications, 2000.

Wagner, C. Peter. *Apostles and Prophets*. Ventura, CA: Regal Books, 2000.

———. *Changing Church*. Ventura, CA: Regal Books, 2004.

———. *Churchquake*. Ventura, CA: Regal Books, 1999.

———. *The New Apostolic Churches*. Ventura, CA: Gospel Light Publications, 2000.

Watson, David. *I Believe in the Church*. Grand Rapids, MI: Wm. B. Eerdmans Pub. Co., 1979.

Williams, J. Rodman. *Renewal Theology*. Grand Rapids, MI: Zondervan, 1996.

———. *The Era of the Spirit*. South Plainfield, NJ: Logos Publishing, 1971.

Yates, Timothy. *The Expansion of Christianity*. Westmont, IL: InterVarsity Press, 2004.

Yeakley Jr., Flavil R. *Discipling Dilemma: A Study of the Discipling Movement Among Churches of Christ*. Nashville, TN: Gospel Advocate Co., 1988.